OVER 201 WORRY –

HCG MAINTENANCE RECIPES

Plus Hints & Tips from Experts

Table of Contents

Get your Special Report: "9 Critical Mistakes Nearly Everybody Makes When Moving into the Maintenance Phase of the HCG Diet…" -- FREE for a limited time!

Congratulations on making the decision to quickly and easily create a new you. With the help of the *Over 201 Worry Free HCG Maintenance Recipes* book, you'll soon be enjoying food you haven't eaten in quite a while…or maybe ever, because the HCG Diet is so amazing. Finally there is a weight loss program that you can stick to and ACTUALLY get results from before you surrender to being hopelessly overweight. To make your transition to maintenance easier, and more convenient, we want to give you our Special Report: "9 *Critical Mistakes Nearly Everybody Makes When Moving into the Maintenance Phase of the HCG Diet*" as our special, free bonus.

It's easy to get this helpful bonus. All you have to do is go to www.HCGDietBooks.com and use the access code: **maint44**

Some of the biggest problems that participants on the HCG diet face are boredom, lack of accurate information, and lack of time required to research the intricacies of this potentially complex diet. Knowledge is the key to completing the HCG diet successfully and maintaining optimum results.

Don't waste any more of your valuable time searching blogs written by people who often know little more about the program than you do, OR looking at knock-off websites selling products with a heaping helping of misinformation. Get your *Special Report: "9 Critical Mistakes Nearly Everybody Makes When Moving into the Maintenance Phase of the HCG Diet…"* NOW at www.**HCGDietBooks.com** today!

Also, when you request this bonus special report online, you'll automatically receive instant discount coupons at some of the HCG World's most respected and highly rated businesses. You'll receive a comprehensive list of links to information and services to make the diet more convenient and less expensive, sample menus for different phases of the diet, and much more! These free bonus gifts will make the HCG diet faster, easier, cheaper, and *better* for you in the long run.

Don't wait - request your bonus online report at **HCGDietBooks.com** and get on the fast track to continue your HCG Diet success story today!

Send us your success story as we would love to see you online. Meanwhile, happy HCGing!

Linda

Dedication

This cook book is dedicated to those of you who have reached the maintenance phase of the HCG Diet Protocol. Congratulations to you! You have completed the rigorous and restrictive very low calorie phase and are ready to continue your journey into the very important maintenance phase, moving toward the rest of your life with your new slimmer body. Many participants feel a strong sense of accomplishment and overall well-being at this point. They are ecstatic due to their substantial amount of weight loss… then a bit of panic sets in. Now what? The list of allowable foods has grown exponentially. "What can I eat on the maintenance phase and going forward so that I don't gain the weight back?" Our mission for this book is to provide you with recipes that are NOT the obvious, boring or tasteless. We set out to give you simple, yet extraordinary recipes, which we are sure you will love during this exciting new phase of the protocol and beyond.

These recipes have been put to the test, both in regard to taste and protocol acceptability. We wish for you exciting, easy, and fun dining experiences while you journey through the maintenance phase (P3). Discover a sense of new found freedom as you assimilate the sound principles set forth by Dr. Simeons that underlie our recipes. With your new knowledge of foods and the recipes in this book, the next few weeks will fly by. Savor both your meals and your success!

Contributors

(In Alphabetic Order)

Beth Brown, coordinator

Sheri Carriger, cook

Christa Prinster, cook

Norma Prinster, cook

Jeni Trent, mixologist

Peggy Walker, cover design

Calvin Walkingstick, photographer

We certainly enjoyed working on this project and

tasting the fruits of our collaborative labor!

Most of the nutritional information including calorie count, fat, carbohydrate, dietary fiber, sugar and protein grams was obtained using the website CalorieCount.com at http://caloriecount.about.com/cc/recipe_analysis.php in September of 2010.

Introduction

If you have just completed the very low calorie phase of the HCG Protocol and are now ready to continue your journey into the next phase known as Maintenance, CONGRATULATIONS! The maintenance phase of the HCG protocol is also known as Phase 3 or P3 from Kevin Trudeau's book, *The Weight Loss Cure "They" Don't Want You to Know About*. During the very low calorie phase of the diet, your main goal was to shed body weight. However, your new goal during the maintenance phase is to maintain your new weight. This is an extremely important part of the HCG Diet Protocol. A bird's eye view of the maintenance phase goals are as follows:

- YOUR GOAL: To create a new weight set point. A set point is a weight that your body automatically maintains, close to your last HCG date weight.
- YOUR BODY'S GOAL: To "recover" the weight you lost. This is a key point that most people are unaware of when they "finish" a diet. Without a method to create a new weight set point, most bodies successfully "recover" the lost weight – sound familiar?
- To ensure that YOUR GOAL wins over YOUR BODY'S GOAL, you must perform the maintenance phase diligently.

Now, let's review a summary of Dr. Simeons' HCG protocol maintenance phase:

Eat what you want, when you want **(preferably when you are hungry, and listen to your body for when you have had enough)** except no sugars and no starches, and weigh EVERYDAY. If you are 2.1 pounds over your last injection (HCG) weight, perform a Steak Day*.

*Steak Day: "Skip breakfast and lunch but take plenty to drink. In the evening, eat a huge steak with only an apple or a raw tomato." - Dr. Simeons

After being on the very low calorie phase of the HCG Protocol, the maintenance phase should feel like the sky is the limit. Try not to get hung up on what you can't have (sugars and starches). Instead, focus on what you can have (pork chops, broccoli, turkey, almonds, etc.). The best plan of action is to "protein up", enjoy some "good-for-you" fats, and eat lots of fresh fruits and a variety of vegetables. You should have caution with dairy, nuts and starchy vegetables, and simply enjoy P3 (Maintenance). It is good to know that many people never "need" a steak day but you can have steak when you like.

For a detailed listing of over 1,000 food and drink items, refer to the General Outline of Beverage/Food Items list in either the *HCG Weight Loss Cure Guide* or the *Pocket Guide to the HCG Protocol*. These list the nutritional information and have an indicator for which phases of the protocol each particular food/drink is allowed. While this information is helpful during the low calorie phase of the diet, it is invaluable during the maintenance phase. The extremely limited list of foods allowed in the very low calorie phase of the diet explodes with possibilities for the maintenance phase. With this knowledge at a your fingertips, you are better equipped to make good food choices, discover healthy tasty foods, and formulate new eating habits, making it not only possible, but probable that your weight loss will be maintained.

We know it can be scary entering the maintenance phase because you go from knowing exactly what to do and when to do it, to Dr. Simeons' one rule: "Eat what you want when you want except no sugars and no starches, but weigh every morning to make sure you stay within 2 pounds of weight as of last injection. If you do go over the 2 pound limit, perform a Steak Day."

So, let's review. During the first 3 weeks of maintenance, remember you should have NO sugars and NO starches. During the second 3 weeks of maintenance you slowly add sugars and starches. "Slowly" is the key word in moving to the later phase with success. It is absolutely imperative that you weigh daily and perform a "steak day" on the very day you weigh more than 2 pounds over your last HCG day. Since healthy eating is as much art as science for many of us, we will go one step further in understanding Dr. Simeons' 'one' rule.

Philosophy of what *is* and *is not* allowed during Maintenance

There are differences of opinion on exactly what Dr. Simeons meant for the first three weeks of maintenance when he said the following: "During this period patients must realize that the so-called carbohydrate, that is sugar, rice, bread, potatoes, pastries etc., are by far the most dangerous. If no carbohydrates whatsoever are eaten, fats can be indulged in somewhat more liberally and even small quantities of alcohol, such as a glass of wine with meals, does no harm…"

And, referring to the first 3 weeks after the very low calorie phase: "For the following 3 weeks, all foods are allowed except starch and sugar in any form (careful with very sweet fruit)." Dr. Simeons

Since small amounts of alcohol, such as a glass of wine with meals, is described to do no harm, we contend that sugar and starch items are items that have a significant amount of carbohydrates and/or sugar, not items that have 4 grams or less, for example, of sugar in a serving. So, while cookies, cakes, candy, etc. are clearly 'sugars', a teaspoon of ketchup on a hamburger does not constitute 'a sugar'. Nor do sweet fruits constitute a sugar, but they must be eaten with caution tempered by the daily weighing.

The same argument exists for starches. While Dr. Simeons mentions items that are obviously considered 'starches', he gives no examples of vegetables that are starchy, such as beans or other vegetables that have protein and fiber. Therefore, we contend that some starchy vegetables (the ones with redeeming benefits of protein and fiber) are allowed in small quantities, with caution.

Other notes or general guidelines we have found to be helpful in maintaining our new weight loss:

In general, you must use caution with 'low fat' food with the exception of dairy products. Low fat and non-fat dairy products such as cheese and milk, are considered healthy alternatives because the products are skimmed after the fat rises to the top during processing and nothing is generally added to make up for that fat. However, the other low fat and non-fat items such as low fat yogurt, mayonnaise, salad dressing, etc., are a different story because many times the removal of fat is often offset by adding sugars, which are not allowed during the 1st three weeks of maintenance.

Obvious selections allowed during maintenance:

Most fruits, most vegetables, and any kind of protein (eggs, beef, chicken, pork, turkey, fish, seafood) are foods generally allowed during the HCG maintenance phase. And, let's face it, we can all come up with a million combinations of these foods when the foods are fixed individually without much imagination. However, our goal with this book was to provide you with the 'not so obvious' and give you variety, without too much thought, for breakfast, snacks, party foods, and combination foods, which usually require much more effort and planning.

Not so obvious selections allowed during maintenance:

To help you think outside the box, especially regarding nutritionally sound sources of protein, consider the following food: elk, ostrich, deer/venison, goat, lamb, bison, Hamachi Kama (neck of Hamachi or Young Yellow tail Tuna), eel, tofu, spirulina*, milk, cheese (less processed: ricotta, mozzarella, goat, mascarpone; more processed: cheddar, Colby, Monterey jack).

*According to Natural Ways (www.naturalways.com/spirul1.htm): "Spirulina is being developed as the "food of the future" because of its amazing ability to synthesize high quality concentrated food more efficiently than any other algae. Most notably, spirulina is 65 to 71 percent complete protein, with all essential amino acids in perfect balance. In comparison, beef is only 22 percent protein." According to experienced users, spirulina can be used in tomato or vegetable juice, frozen yogurt, yogurt, apple sauce, shakes, and smoothies. The most popular way to enjoy spirulina is to add it to your favorite fruit or vegetable juice in a blender. Spirulina can be quickly drunk in just plain distilled water for maximum absorption and health benefits, but don't expect this method to taste good. To incorporate spirulina into your life for extra nutrition, try adding it to soups, salads, pasta, and breads, but keep in mind those nutrients can be lost at high temperatures.

Vegetarian Notes

As alluded to throughout the HCG protocol, protein seems to be quite helpful with healthy weight maintenance. Although we have included some great vegetarian recipes in the book, this is our further attempt to give more direction to vegetarians and vegans by gathering the following list of higher protein foods. These are 'higher' protein foods, exclusive of meats, which have significantly higher protein per portion than most of the items listed below. This list is intended to help you add variety and give you direction in finding more great recipes using online searches and other resources based on key ingredients.

Relatively high sources of protein in the different food groups:

Nuts and nut products: These items are caution items on the maintenance phase of the HCG Diet Protocol due to the relatively high fat and relatively high carbohydrate nutritional values. These include almonds, almond milk, cashews, peanuts, peanut butter, sunflower seeds, pecans, pumpkin seeds, walnuts, etc.

Vegetable foods/drinks: artichokes (4g), asparagus (5g), baked beans (12g), black beans (15g), black-eyed/cowpeas/garbanzo (15g), great northern (14g), kidney beans (13g), lima beans (12g), mung beans (3g), navy beans (15g), pinto beans (14g), soybeans (22g – 26g), white beans (19), beet greens (4g), broccoli (4g), corn* (4g), lentils (17g), peas (8g), potato*(5g), soymilk (6g), soy yogurt (5), spinach (6g), tempeh (15), tofu (13), veggie burger (5)

Grains: buckwheat oats* (6g), bulgar* (6g), cornmeal* (10g), noodles* (3g), egg bagel*(10g), flax* (5g), oat bran, cooked (7g), oat bran (8g), quinoa, cooked (11g), white rice*, cooked (5g), seitan* (26g), spaghetti* (7g), wheat flour* (13g)

*These foods and drinks have significant protein, but too many carbs in a serving to be allowed during the 1st 3 weeks of maintenance.

Finally, to aid in your success, this book features tips, hints and common concerns that will help you make the next weeks of your life exciting, easy, and fun. Our best recipe to date is simply inspired by the HCG protocol:

Start fresh and healthy…

End delicious and thin…

Now that's a recipe worth following!

Some of our Favorites to Look Forward to:

The following are great food item choices that you can look forward to for the **2nd Three Weeks of Maintenance** as they are starches. The items are high in both protein and fiber, but just a little too high in carbohydrates to make the cut for the 1st three weeks of maintenance:

Low carb/high protein and/or high fiber tortillas like Mission – Carb Balance
Ezekiel bread

Some of our favorite recipes that don't quite make the cut for the 1st Three Weeks of Maintenance, but can be integrated beginning the **2nd Three Weeks of Maintenance,** when starches and sugars are slowly added back into a participant's diet follow:

Spicy Black Bean Salsa
Taco Chips
Crazy Hi-Protein Chicken Wrap
Cheesy Chicken
Mashed Sweet Potatoes
Festive Sweet Potato Casserole
Pecan Pie
Creamy Chocolate Pie
Chocolate Peanut Butter Fluff

Sweeteners:

Review the chart below for sweeteners allowed during the different phases of maintenance. Some notes to keep in mind when choosing alternative sweeteners for different applications:
Some are considered healthy; others are not. Some taste very much like white sugar; others do not. Some have aftertaste; others do not. Some cause minor to major discomfort in some participants, i.e. bloating, intestinal turmoil, and more to varying degrees. Some sweeteners work significantly better for baking vs. sweetening drinks vs. sprinkled directly on food.

Please pay attention to the differences and find one or more that work for you. This definitely varies from one person to the next, but it will be to your benefit to do some experimenting and find a couple that you prefer to work with, for example, for cooking vs. baking vs. drinking, etc. Many people use 2-3 different types of sweetener on a daily basis because of the above notes. Liquid stevia works well for drinks (iced tea, lemonade), stevia packets or Splenda work well directly on salads (fruit salad, chicken salad), and Lakanto or others work better for baking. Personal preference is quite varied.

Sweeteners	Serving Size	Calories	Pro	Carb	Fiber	Sugar	Fat	1st 3 wks	2nd 3 wks	Life
agave nectar (lower glycemic index and takes less than sugar)	1 tsp	15	0	4	0	4	0	Δ	Δ	Y
aspartame: NutraSweet, Equal	1 serving	0	0	<1	0	0	0	Y	Y	Y
brown sugar, unpacked	1 tsp	11	0	3	0	3	0	N	Δ	Y
cane sugar, organic, unrefined	1 tsp	16	0	4	0	4	0	N	Δ	Y
corn syrup, light or dark	1 tsp	19-20	0	5	0	2	0	N	Δ	Y
fructose, dry	1 tsp	15	0	4	0	4	0	N	Δ	Y
honey	1 tsp	21	0	6	0	5	0	N	Δ	Y
Lakanto (all-natural), fermented Erythritol, Luo Han Guo	1 tsp	0	0	4	0	0	0	Y	Y	Y
maple syrup, molasses, light/dark	1 tsp	17-20	0	4-5	0	4-5	0	N	Δ	Y
powdered sugar	1 tsp	10	0	2	0	2	0	N	Δ	Y
saccharin: Sweet'N Low, Sugar Twin, and Necta Sweet	1 serving	0	0	<1	0	0	0	Y	Y	Y
sorghum syrup	1 tsp	17	0	4	0	4	0	N	Δ	Y
stevia	1 packet	0	0	1	0	0	0	Y	Y	Y
sucralose: 0 Calorie Splenda	1 serving	0	0	<1	0	0	0	Y	Y	Y
sucralose: Baking Blend Splenda	1 tsp	20	0	4	0	4	0	N	Y	Y
Sugar Twin	1 packet	0	0	<1	0	0	0	Y	Y	Y
white sugar	1 tsp	16	0	4	0	4	0	N	Δ	Y

Beverages

Almond Shake

2 cups ice
½ cup half and half
1 tablespoon ground almond
½ cup skim milk
¾ teaspoon DaVinci Gourmet Sugar Free Almond Syrup
¾ teaspoon DaVinci Gourmet Sugar Free Hazelnut Syrup

Combine ingredients in a blender and blend on high until smooth.

Yield: 2 servings
Per Serving: Calories: 117; Fat: 8.5 g; Carbs: 6.3 g; Dietary Fiber: 0.4 g; Sugar: 3.3 g; Protein 4.5 g

Simple Fruit & Protein Shake

½ cup skim milk
¼ cup low fat 2% cottage cheese
½ cup blueberries or strawberries
1 scoop vanilla protein powder
Ice cubes

Blend all ingredients in blender and serve.

Yield: 1 serving
Per Serving: Calories: 254; Fat: 3.4 g; Carbs: 22.6 g; Dietary Fiber: 1.7 g; Sugar: 16.7 g; Protein: 33.4 g

> **Healthy Tip:** When it comes to eating, avoid being spontaneous. Have a stash of pre-approved foods you know are healthy for you on hand in your purse, car, desk drawer, etc.

Cinnamon Cottage Cheese Smoothie

½ cup low fat 2% cottage cheese
¼ cup skim milk
¼ teaspoon cinnamon
0 calorie sweetener of choice to taste

Combine cottage cheese, milk and cinnamon in blender. Blend until smooth. Add 0 calorie sweetener of choice. Serve immediately.

Yield: 1 serving
Per Serving: Calories: 124; Fat: 2.2 g; Carbs: 8.6 g; Dietary Fiber: 0.3 g; Sugar: 3.5 g; Protein: 17.6 g

Spirulina Sunrise Shake

½ cup frozen chunks of mango
½ cup raspberries
½ cup light cranberry juice
1 teaspoon Earthrise Spirulina (Earthrise brand has good reviews.)

Blend with ice and serve.

Yield: 1 serving
Per Serving: Calories: 116; Fat: 0.6 g; Carbs: 26.4 g; Dietary Fiber: 5.5 g; Sugar: 19.9 g; Protein: 3.2 g

> *Lifestyle Tip:* Don't depend on willpower forever – that's not how we're built.

Dessert Fudge Shake

½ cup low fat 2% cottage cheese
1 scoop chocolate protein powder
0 calorie sweetener of choice to taste
1 cup ice
½ cup water
1 tablespoon walnuts

Place all ingredients except nuts in blender and blend for 30 seconds. Open the lid and add the walnuts. Chop in blender for a few seconds.

Yield: 1 serving
Per Serving: Calories: 232; Fat: 7.9 g; Carbs: 8.9 g; Dietary Fiber: 1.3 g; Sugar: 2.0 g; Protein: 32.4 g

Healthy Chocolate Shake

1 scoop chocolate protein powder
2 tablespoons whole flax seeds
½ cup low fat 2% cottage cheese
1 cup ice
Dash clear or chocolate stevia

Place all ingredients in a blender and blend on high for about one minute or until all the flax seeds have been ground.

Yield: 1 serving
Per Serving: Calories: 259; Fat: 9.2 g; Carbs: 11.1 g; Dietary Fiber: 4.6 g; Sugar: 2.1 g; Protein: 33.1 g

Fruit Shake

1 cup fresh or frozen berries (blueberries, strawberries, raspberries, etc. or a mixture thereof)
1 scoop vanilla or strawberry protein powder
1 cup ice
½ cup low fat 2% cottage cheese
½ cup skim milk
0 calorie sweetener of choice to taste

Combine all ingredients in a blender and blend on high for 30 seconds.

Yield: 2 servings
Per Serving: Calories: 155; Fat: 2.4 g; Carbs: 13.1 g; Dietary Fiber: 1.4 g; Sugar: 8.3 g; Protein: 20.8 g

Quick Spirulina Breakfast Drink

2 teaspoons spirulina (Earthrise brand has good reviews.)
½ cup light apple juice
1 peach, pear, apple, or 1 cup of berries
6 drops vanilla crème stevia

Blend well.

Yield: 1 serving
Per Serving: Calories: 88; Fat: 0.3 g; Carbs: 16.9 g; Dietary Fiber: 1.5 g; Sugar: 15.2 g; Protein: 4.9 g

> *Lifestyle Tip:* Be specific with your goals listing dates, goal weights and detailed ongoing actions such as exercising regularly, etc.

Spirulina Veggie Drink

1 tablespoon spirulina (Earthrise brand has good reviews.)
1 cup V8 Juice

Blend well.

Optional: Herbs such as parsley, cumin, dill weed, or cayenne for flavoring. These do not add to nutritional value.

Yield: 1 serving
Per Serving: Calories: 81; Fat: 0.6 g; Carbs: 11.6 g; Dietary Fiber: 2.0 g; Sugar: 8.1 g; Protein: 7.1 g

Soy Milk Fruit Shake

1 cup soy milk
½ cup nonfat Greek yogurt
½ cup frozen unsweetened sliced peaches
¼ cup frozen unsweetened red raspberries
0 calorie sweetener of choice equal to ¼ cup sugar or to taste
½ teaspoon vanilla extract
¼ teaspoon almond extract
Fresh mint (optional)

Place all ingredients in blender. Cover with lid. Process until smooth. Add ice for desired consistency. Serve immediately in tall glasses. Garnish with mint, if desired.

Yield: 2 servings
Per Serving: Calories: 128; Fat: 2.4 g; Carbs: 19.1 g; Dietary Fiber: 2.4 g; Sugar: 11.7 g; Protein: 10.5g

Peppermint Patty Shake

½ cup vanilla low fat yogurt
2 scoops chocolate protein
Peppermint stevia
2 cups ice

Combine all ingredients in a blender and blend on high until smooth.

Yield: 2 servings
Per Serving: Calories: 219; Fat: 4.0 g; Carbs: 10.3 g; Dietary Fiber: 0.0 g; Sugar: 8.8 g; Protein: 33.7 g

Peanut Butter Shake

1 scoop chocolate protein powder

2 tablespoons fat free half and half

2 tablespoons Smucker's Natural Peanut Butter

2 ounces cream cheese

0 calorie sweetener of choice equal to 2 tablespoons sugar or to taste

1 teaspoon vanilla extract

1 cup water

2 cups ice

Put all ingredients in blender and blend until smooth.

Yield: 2 servings
Per Serving: Calories: 225; Fat: 15.3 g; Carbs: 8.7 g; Dietary Fiber: 1.3 g; Sugar: 4.4 g; Protein: 14.3 g

⚠️ The caution sign identifies recipes that include caution items as ingredients. Some high fat caution items are milk, cheese, and nuts. Some high sugar (even though natural sugar) are pineapple and banana. Some high starchy vegetables are black beans and other legumes. These items are caution items for the 1st 3 weeks of maintenance. **Use these recipes in moderation and watch your morning weight closely, particularly during the 1st 3 weeks.**

Café de Almendra (Almond Coffee)

1 scoop chocolate protein powder

2 tablespoons fat free half and half

2 ounces ⅓ less fat cream cheese

2 tablespoons chopped almonds

1 tablespoon instant coffee

1 tablespoon chocolate sugar free syrup

1 teaspoon vanilla extract

0 calorie sweetener of choice equal to 4 teaspoons sugar

1 cup cold coffee

2 cups ice

Put all ingredients in blender and blend on high speed until smooth.

Yield: 2 servings
Per Serving: Calories: 186; Fat: 10.0 g; Carbs: 8.3 g; Dietary Fiber: 0.8 g; Sugar: 4.0 g; Protein: 13.9 g

Peaches and Cream Smoothie

1 cup 2% milk
2 tablespoons sugar free, fat free vanilla pudding
½ cup ice
½ peach

Place all ingredients in a blender and blend until smooth.

Yield: 1 serving
Per Serving: Calories: 133; Fat: 2.7 g; Carbs: 22.8 g; Dietary Fiber: 0.9 g; Sugar: 10.4 g; Protein: 4.6 g

Strawberry (or other fruit) Shake

½ cup 2% milk
½ cup strawberries
2 tablespoons DaVinci Gourmet Sugar Free Vanilla Syrup
5 ice cubes

Put all ingredients into a blender and blend until smooth.

Yield: 1 serving
Per Serving: Calories: 84; Fat: 2.6 g; Carbs: 11.2 g; Dietary Fiber: 1.4 g; Sugar: 9.7 g; Protein: 4.5 g

Orange and Vanilla Smoothie

1 cup skim milk
½ cup low fat 2% cottage cheese
Orange stevia
1 scoop vanilla protein powder
2 cups ice

Put all ingredients into a blender and blend on high speed until smooth.

Yield: 2 servings
Per Serving: Calories: 172; Fat: 4.5 g; Carbs: 9.8 g; Dietary Fiber: 0.0 g; Sugar: 7.9 g; Protein: 22.3 g

Activity Tip: Write down 25 activities that you like to do or that you used to like to do. Doing things you like is much more effective than trying to force yourself to do activities, such as exercise, that you don't like to do.

©Over 201 Worry-Free HCG Maintenance Recipe   14

Cheesecake Shake

1½ cups water
1 cup fat free cottage cheese
1 tablespoon peanut butter
1 package sugar free, fat free vanilla pudding mix
2 cups ice

Put all ingredients into a blender and blend on high speed until smooth.

Yield: 2 servings
Per Serving: Calories: 175; Fat: 6.3 g; Carbs: 11.9 g; Dietary Fiber: 0.6 g; Sugar: 1.2 g; Protein: 17.6 g

Berry Smoothie

¼ cup 2% milk
¼ cup 2% fat Greek yogurt
¼ cup blueberries
¼ cup strawberries or raspberries
¼ cup ice
0 calorie sweetener of choice equal to 4 teaspoons sugar or to taste
1 tablespoon flaxseed (optional – included in nutritional information)

Put all ingredients into a blender and blend until smooth.

Yield: 1 serving
Per Serving: Calories: 137; Fat: 5.5 g; Carbs: 17.2 g; Dietary Fiber: 3.5 g; Sugar: 10.8 g; Protein: 8.6 g

Iced Caramel Macchiato

1 scoop chocolate protein powder
1 cup strong brewed coffee, cooled
2 cups ice
2 tablespoons DaVinci Gourmet Sugar Free Carmel Syrup

Place all ingredients in a blender and blend until smooth.

Yield: 1 serving
Per Serving: Calories: 85; Fat: 1.2 g; Carbs: 3.0 g; Dietary Fiber: 0.8 g; Sugar: 1.5 g; Protein: 15.3 g

Strawberry Cheesecake Shake

½ cup 2% milk
1 tablespoon cheesecake sugar free, fat free pudding mix
½ cup frozen strawberries

Place all ingredients in a blender and blend until smooth.

Yield: 1 serving
Per Serving: Calories: 110; Fat: 2.7 g; Carbs: 17.5 g; Dietary Fiber: 1.5 g; Sugar: 9.8 g; Protein: 4.6 g

Nutrition Tip: Understand that there are bad and good carbs. Learn the good carbs from the bad ones. Good: whole grains, vegetables and fruit. Bad or not-so-good: white foods such as things made with white flour, white sugar, white pasta, and white rice. Other not-so-good carbs: candy, cakes and sugary drinks. To improve health and lose weight, eliminate or limit bad carbs.

Beverages – Alcoholic

Jack and Diet Coke

1½ ounces Jack Daniels
Diet coke

Mix ingredients, serve over ice. Enjoy!

Yield: 1 serving
Per Serving: Calories: 110; Fat: 0.6 g; Carbs: 0.4 g; Dietary Fiber: 0.0 g; Sugar: 0.0 g; Protein: 0.0 g

Pitcher of Margaritas

Blender full of ice
3/4 cup tequila
6 tablespoons lime juice
2 tablespoons lemon juice
¼ teaspoon orange extract
0 calorie sweetener of choice equal to ½ cup sugar
½ cup water
1 egg white

Put egg white into blender and blend until frothy. Add all ingredients, except ice and continue to blend. Add ice until desired consistency.

Yield: 4 servings   Serving Size: 1 cup
Per Serving: Calories: 109; Fat: 0.0 g; Carbs: 6.7 g; Dietary Fiber: 0.1 g; Sugar: 0.7 g; Protein: 1.0 g

Thin Cape Cod

1½ ounces vodka
6 ounces diet cranberry juice i.e. Ocean Spray, Langer's, Compliments, President's Choice, Snapple

Pour both ingredients into glass and stir. Garnish with a lime wedge.

Yield: 1 serving
Per Serving: Calories: 102; Fat: 0.0 g; Carbs: 1.4 g; Dietary Fiber: 0.0 g; Sugar: 1.4 g; Protein: 0.0 g

Thin Screwdriver

1½ ounces vodka
6 ounces light orange juice i.e. Minute Maid Light, Tropicana Light 'N Healthy

Pour over a glass of ice, mix and enjoy!

Yield: 1 serving
Per Serving: Calories: 145; Fat: 0.0 g; Carbs: 12.3 g; Dietary Fiber: 0.0 g; Sugar: 9.5 g; Protein: 1.0 g

Thin Vodka Chiller

1½ ounces vodka
8 ounces diet ginger ale i.e. Canada Dry, Schweppes, President's Choice, etc.

Garnish with lime.

Yield: 1 serving
Per Serving: Calories: 98; Fat: 0.0 g; Carbs: 0.0 g; Dietary Fiber: 0.0 g; Sugar: 0.0 g; Protein: 0.0 g

Bloody Mary

⅔ cup tomato juice
6 shakes Worcestershire sauce
1½ teaspoons lemon juice
1½ ounces vodka
Splash pickle juice
Dash celery salt

Mix the first 5 ingredients together in order listed. Add celery salt and pour over ice.

Yield: 1 serving
Per Serving: Calories: 133; Fat: 0.1 g; Carbs: 8.6 g; Dietary Fiber: 0.7 g; Sugar: 7.0 g; Protein: 1.3 g

Perfect Vodka Martini

1½ ounces vodka
¾ ounce dry vermouth
¾ ounce sweet vermouth
1 green olive

Pour the vodka and the vermouths into a mixing glass filled with cubed ice. Stir for 30 seconds. Strain mixture into a chilled martini glass. Garnish with green olive.

Yield: 1 serving
Per Serving: Calories: 150; Fat: 0.0 g; Carbs: 1.6 g; Dietary Fiber: 0.1 g; Sugar: 0.0 g; Protein: 0.0 g

Egg Nog

2 eggs, yolks separated from whites
0 calorie sweetener of choice equal to 2 ½ tablespoons sugar
2 cups 2% milk
½ cup heavy whipping cream
½ teaspoon nutmeg
¼ teaspoon cinnamon
1 teaspoon vanilla
3 ounces bourbon or rum, your preference
1 tablespoon of sugar

Non cooking method: Beat the egg yolks until eggs lighten in color. Slowly add the sweetener until dissolved. Add the milk, cream, nutmeg, bourbon or rum.

Cooking Method (optional to avoid consuming raw egg): Mix ingredients except rum or bourbon in blender. Cook mixture over low heat until it is of a consistency to coat the back of a spoon. Make sure to stir constantly to avoid scorching. Remove from heat, stir in the rum or bourbon, put in mixing bowl and refrigerate while doing the next step.

To finish with either method: In a separate bowl, beat the egg whites until soft peaks form. With the mixer still running, gradually add 1 tablespoon of sugar and beat until stiff peaks form. Whisk the egg whites into the mixture. Chill and serve with a dash of nutmeg on top.

Yield: 1 serving   Serving Size: ½ cup
Per Serving: Calories: 130; Fat: 5.4 g; Carbs: 7.6 g; Dietary Fiber: 0.0 g; Sugar: 6.4 g; Protein: 5.1 g

Thin Cosmo

1 jigger (1½ ounces or 3 tablespoons) citrus or regular vodka
2 tablespoons diet cranberry juice OR 2 teaspoons unsweetened cranberry juice and
    2 tablespoons water
1 tablespoon fresh lime juice
2 to 3 drops orange extract
0 calorie sweetener of choice equal to 1 tablespoon sugar

Put the ingredients in a cocktail shaker half full of ice. Shake well. Taste for sweetness if using unsweetened cranberry juice, which is highly variable. You may need to add more 0 calorie sweetener of choice. Strain into a martini glass. Garnish with a small lime wedge or curl of lime peel.

Yield: 1 serving
Per Serving: Calories: 103; Fat: 0.0 g; Carbs: 3.0 g; Dietary Fiber: 0.1 g; Sugar: 0.5 g; Protein: 0.1 g

Brandy Sangaree

½ teaspoon powdered sugar
1 teaspoon water
2 ounces brandy
3 ounces carbonated water
½ ounce port wine
Dash nutmeg
Dash cinnamon

Mix powdered sugar and 1 teaspoon of water until dissolved. Add brandy and pour into a highball glass filled with cubed ice. Add carbonated water and stir. 'Float' the port wine on top. Sprinkle the nutmeg and cinnamon on top.

Yield: 1 serving
Per Serving: Calories: 145; Fat: 0.1 g; Carbs: 2.0 g; Dietary Fiber: 0.2 g; Sugar: 1.4 g; Protein: 0.0 g

Gin and Ginger Ale (Gin Buck)

1 ½ ounces gin
1 tablespoon lemon or lime juice, fresh squeezed preferred
6 ounces diet ginger ale i.e. Canada Dry, Vernor's, Hanson's
Ice

Combine all ingredients. Pour into glass with cubed ice.

Yield: 1 serving
Per Serving: Calories: 116; Fat: 0.0 g; Carbs: 1.2 g; Dietary Fiber: 0.4 g; Sugar: 0.3 g; Protein: 0.2 g

> *Tasty Tip:* To avoid dilution by melting water ice cubes, make ice cubes with the filler ingredient i.e. diet ginger ale or diet tonic water. Simply fill an empty ice cube tray and let the cubes freeze. It only takes a couple of hours and makes a big difference if you are a slow drinker.

Gin and Tonic

4 ounces diet tonic water i.e. Schweppes, Canada Dry
2 ounces gin
Slice of lime
Ice

Pour the gin and the tonic water into a tall, chilled highball glass filled with ice cubes. Stir well. Garnish with the lime.

Yield: 1 serving
Per Serving: Calories: 150; Fat: 0.0 g; Carbs: 0.2 g; Dietary Fiber: 0.0 g; Sugar: 0.0 g; Protein: 0.0 g

Irish Coffee

1 ounce Irish whiskey
1 – 2 tablespoons Da Vinci Sugar Free Irish Crème Syrup
8 ounces fresh brewed hot coffee
2 tablespoons ready whip topping
Dash of nutmeg

Mix whiskey, syrup and coffee. Top with whip cream and a dash of nutmeg.

Yield: 1 serving
Per Serving: Calories: 117; Fat: 4.7 g; Carbs: 0.5 g; Dietary Fiber: 0 g; Sugar: 0.1 g; Protein: 0.6 g

Long Island Iced Tea

2 tablespoons lemon juice, fresh squeezed preferred
¼ cup water
0 calorie sweetener of choice equal to ¼ cup sugar
1 ounce gin
1 ounce tequila
1 ounce vodka
1 ounce rum
1 ounce sugar free triple sec i.e. Monino Sugar Free Triple Sec
Splash diet cola
Ice

Mix lemon juice, water, and sweetener to create the sour mix. Add the rest of the ingredients and shake briefly. Pour over full glasses of ice.

Yield: 2 servings
Per Serving: Calories: 150; Fat: 0.3 g; Carbs: 5.7 g; Dietary Fiber: 0.1 g; Sugar: 0.7 g; Protein: 0.9 g

Skinny Strawberry Daiquiri

Either ½ cup sliced strawberries and a small handful of ice
        OR
½ cup of frozen sliced strawberries
1 tablespoon lime juice
1 jigger rum (1 ½ ounces)
0 calorie sweetener of choice to taste

Blend all ingredients.

Yield: 1 serving
Per Serving: Calories: 104; Fat: 0.0 g; Carbs: 2.8 g; Dietary Fiber: 0.2 g; Sugar: 0.6 g; Protein: 0.1 g

Mojito

2 wedges of juicy lime
6 medium sized mint leaves roughly torn
0 calorie sweetener of choice equal to 1 tablespoon sugar
2 ounces dry white rum
Crushed ice, preferred, cubes will work also
Top off with club soda

Place 4 mint leaves, sweetener, and a wedge of lime in a tall highball glass. Muddle the ingredients in the glass, preferably with a wooden utensil. How to muddle: push down the utensil with a firm, slow twisting action. Be careful not to break down the ingredients into mush or bits. Crushing or piercing is not the goal; think bruise and press. Caution: Not enough muddling will leave you with a drink that seems like a waste of time and too much muddling may release bitterness from the fruit and herbs. The goal is to release essential oils, juice, and the rich flavors but not make mashed ingredients.

Add rum and stir well to dissolve the sweetener. Pour over ice and top off with diet club soda. Stir lightly, garnish with mint and lime wedge.

Yield: 1 serving
Per Serving: Calories: 135; Fat: 0.0 g; Carbs: 2.8 g; Dietary Fiber: 0.1 g; Sugar: 0.3 g; Protein: 0 .1 g

Vodka and Diet Tonic

1½ ounces vodka
8 ounces diet tonic water i.e. Schweppes, President's Choice, Lowes, etc.

Mix ingredients and serve over ice.

Yield: 1 serving
Per Serving: Calories: 98; Fat: 0.0 g; Carbs: 0.0 g; Dietary Fiber: 0.0 g; Sugar: 0.0 g; Protein: 0.0 g

Margarita

1 jigger (1 ½ ounces) tequila
2 tablespoons lime juice, fresh preferred
¼ cup water
¼ teaspoon orange extract
0 calorie sweetener of choice equal to ⅛ cup sugar or to taste
Ice - small handful
Margarita salt or kosher salt

Wet the rim of the glass with lime rind and dip into a small plate of salt. Combine all ingredients. Serves well over ice cubes or mixed in the blender.

Yield: 1 serving
Per Serving: Calories: 117; Fat: 0.0 g; Carbs: 8.8 g; Dietary Fiber: 0.1 g; Sugar: 0.7 g; Protein: 0.1 g

Other quick low carb substitutes for alcoholic drinks

- Gin or vodka and diet tonic
- Scotch and diet soda
- Skinny seven and seven (Seagram's 7 and Diet 7-Up)
- Rum and diet cola
- Rye and ginger (rye whiskey and diet ginger ale)

Other flavoring possibilities for alcohol, coffee, and other drinks are using sugar-free syrups such as DaVinci or Torino brand. The amount of sweetness in them is about equal to the volume -- for example, a teaspoon has about the sweetness of a teaspoon of sugar. These syrups come in an array of sugar free flavors, including some liqueurs – Sugar Free Amaretto, Sugar Free Kahlua, Sugar Free Crème de Menthe, and Sugar Free Irish Cream.

Breakfasts

Spinach Omelet

½ large garlic clove, minced
1 ½ cups pre-washed spinach
4 large egg whites
Crushed red pepper to taste
1 ½ large Roma tomatoes, chopped
¼ cup grated pepper jack cheese

Lightly coat a medium skillet with non-stick cooking spray. Heat on medium, add garlic and cook until fragrant. Add in spinach and cook until soft. Coat a separate skillet lightly with cooking spray and scramble the egg whites. When almost finished, sprinkle in a moderate amount of crushed red pepper, depending on your taste. Top with tomatoes and cheese and serve.

Yield: 1 serving
Per Serving: Calories: 223; Fat: 10.1 g; Carbs: 10.7 g; Dietary Fiber: 3.2 g; Sugar: 6.2 g; Protein: 24.4 g

2nd Three Weeks Option:
Wrap ingredients in 2 6" or 8" Carb Balance Tortillas or Ezekiel Tortillas before topping with tomatoes and cheese.

Yield: 1 serving
Per Serving: Calories: 303; Fat: 12.1 g; Carbs: 22.7 g; Dietary Fiber: 11.2 g; Sugar: 6.2 g; Protein: 27.4 g

Strawberry Cottage Cheese

2 cups low fat 2% cottage cheese
1 small box sugar free strawberry Jell-O
½ cup boiling water

Bring water to a boil, add Jell-O and stir until dissolved. Let cool to room temperature. Put in blender with cottage cheese and blend until smooth. Chill for 2 hours. Serve with fresh strawberries.

Yield: 8 servings   Serving Size: ⅓ cup
Per Serving: Calories: 61; Fat: 1.1 g; Carbs: 2.1 g; Dietary Fiber: 0.0 g; Sugar: 0.2 g; Protein: 9.8 g

Peanut Butter Delight

1 cup low fat 2% cottage cheese
1 tablespoon peanut butter
0 calorie sweetener of choice equal to 1 tablespoon sugar

Stir together cottage cheese and peanut butter. Microwave on high for one minute and then add 0 calorie sweetener of choice. Stir together well.

Yield: 2 servings   Serving Size: ½ cup
Per Serving: Calories: 149; Fat: 6.2 g; Carbs: 6.4 g; Dietary Fiber: 0.5 g; Sugar: 1.1 g; Protein: 17.5 g

Waffles

½ cup Carbquick
1 egg
½ teaspoon vanilla
½ tablespoon sour cream
1 tablespoon butter
4 teaspoons water
0 calorie sweetener of choice equal to 2 teaspoons sugar

Spray waffle iron with non-stick spray or coat with olive oil. Pour ¼ cup batter on waffle iron and cook until done.
Options: Top with our toppings or sugar free syrup.

Yield: 2 servings   Serving Size: ½ batter
Per Serving: Calories: 159; Fat: 13.1 g; Carbs: 12.9 g; Dietary Fiber: 10.5 g; Sugar: 0.0 g; Protein: 7.4 g

⚠ The caution sign identifies recipes that include caution items as ingredients. Some high fat caution items are milk, cheese, and nuts. Some high sugar (even though natural sugar) are pineapple and banana. Some high starchy vegetables are black beans and other legumes. These items are caution items for the 1st 3 weeks of maintenance. **Use these recipes in moderation and watch your morning weight closely, particularly during the 1st 3 weeks.**

Berries and Cream

1 cup fresh berries (blackberries, blueberries, raspberries, strawberries, whatever is in season)
½ cup 2% milk or cream
 0 calorie sweetener of choice equal to taste

Place berries of your choice in a bowl; add milk and 0 calorie sweetener of choice to taste. Enjoy!

Yield: 1 serving
Per Serving: Calories: 123; Fat: 3.1 g; Carbs: 20.6 g; Dietary Fiber: 7.6 g; Sugar: 13.2 g; Protein: 6.0 g

Apple Pancakes

1 medium apple, chopped finely
¼ teaspoon cinnamon
0 calorie sweetener of choice equal to 2 teaspoons sugar

Pancake batter:
¼ cup almond flour
2 egg whites
1 tablespoon water
Dash of sea salt
0 calorie sweetener of choice equal to 1 teaspoon sugar
¼ teaspoon cinnamon
¼ teaspoon vanilla

Finely chop apple, add ¼ teaspoon cinnamon and 0 calorie sweetener of choice and mix thoroughly. In a separate bowl, combine all pancake batter ingredients and mix until smooth. Fold in apple mixture to coat evenly. Spray non-stick pan and prepare like a regular pancake.

Yield: 2 servings
Per Serving: Calories: 134; Fat: 7.2 g; Carbs: 14.2 g; Dietary Fiber: 3.4 g; Sugar: 8.0 g; Protein: 6.8 g

---

Healthy Tip: Take a multi-mineral/multi-vitamin daily.

Breakfast Cheese Spread (Use with Flax Seed Flatbread)

Flax Seed Bread (see recipe and nutrition facts)
¼ cup low fat 2% cottage cheese
¼ cup fresh raspberries
0 calorie sweetener of choice equal to 2 teaspoons sugar
Cinnamon

Slice of flax-seed flatbread featured in this book, spread with cottage cheese. Heat in toaster oven until the cheese starts to melt. Sprinkle with 0 calorie sweetener of choice and cinnamon and top with raspberries.

Yield: 1 serving
Per Serving: Calories: 68; Fat: 1.3 g; Carbs: 7.2 g; Dietary Fiber: 2.3 g; Sugar: 1.6 g; Protein: 8.2 g

Greek Yogurt - What's the difference?

Greek yogurt is thick like sour cream and creamy without additives like xantham gum and pectin. Greek yogurt (plain) has great things like high protein, calcium, and probiotic cultures that aid digestion. Warning: Greek yogurt is expensive, but worth the nutritional value to many 'addicts'. Brands: Oikos, Voskos (reported some bitterness), Fage, Trader Joe's brand, Dannon Greek and Chobani are established brands. The ones we tried were delicious, creamy and very thick. Fage and Oikos taste very similar. Trader Joe's was slightly tangier, which some may prefer and some may not. Generally, 1 cup of Greek yogurt has about 120 calories, 6-9 total carbs, 0 Fiber, and 23 g protein. We tried all 0% fat and were very happy with the taste, so we didn't even try the higher fat content, but we are sure they would be delicious also. The bottom line: the nutritional values are significantly different, with regular yogurt having significantly higher carbs/sugars, more additives and low protein compared to Greek yogurt having significantly less carbs/sugars, less additives and significantly higher protein, which are all good qualities. So, we declare Greek yogurt the clear winner, especially for people trying to maintain a healthy weight or lose weight.

Quick and Delicious Greek

1 teaspoon sugar free, fat free pudding mix
6 ounces 0% fat Greek yogurt
0 calorie sweetener of choice to taste
½ cup strawberries or any fresh or frozen fruit i.e. mixed berries, peaches, etc.

Other serving suggestions, as the list is endless: 1 teaspoon any flavor sugar free gelatin, 1 teaspoon sugar free, fat free pudding mix, any fresh or frozen fruits, any nuts, any sugar free flavoring or extract, such as almond extract or sugar free syrups, etc.

Yield: 1 serving

Per Serving: Calories: 130; Fat: 0.2 g; Carbs: 15.1 g; Dietary Fiber: 1.5 g; Sugar: 10.5 g; Protein: 18.5 g

2nd Three Weeks Option: Honey is a highly preferred sweetener for Greek yogurt lovers, so keep that in mind for the 2nd three weeks and after. Replace 0 calorie sweetener of choice with 1 teaspoon honey.

Yield: 1 serving

Per Serving: Calories: 151; Fat: 0.2 g; Carbs: 19.9 g; Dietary Fiber: 1.5 g; Sugar: 16.3 g; Protein: 18.5 g

Cheesecake Yogurt

1 teaspoon cheesecake sugar free, fat free pudding mix
1 tablespoon cool whip
6 ounces 0% fat Greek yogurt

Blend and enjoy.
Option: Some chopped strawberries or other fresh or frozen fruit.

Yield: 1 serving

Per Serving: Calories: 119; Fat: 1.0 g; Carbs: 9.5 g; Dietary Fiber: 0.0 g; Sugar: 7.9 g; Protein: 18.1 g

Good Morning Peppers

4 ounces breakfast sausage
4 ounces lean ground beef
½ cup chopped onion
¼ cup shredded cheese
4 large beaten eggs
2 red bell peppers

Preheat oven to 350° F. In a skillet, cook sausage and ground beef; drain off all fat and let cool. Line a baking sheet with foil. Cut peppers in half lengthwise. Remove seeds and cut away rib. Combine onion, cheese and eggs with prepared meat. Fill each pepper with meat mixture and place on baking sheet. Bake for 25-30 minutes. Serve hot.

Yield: 4 servings   Serving Size: ½ filled pepper
Per Serving: Calories: 271; Fat: 17.3 g; Carbs: 5.0 g; Dietary Fiber: 1.5 g; Sugar: 3.1 g; Protein: 22.6 g

Almond Flour Pancakes

1 cup almond flour
2 eggs
¼ cup water (for puffier pancakes, you can use sparkling water)
2 tablespoons olive oil
¼ teaspoon sea salt
0 calorie sweetener of choice equal to 1 tablespoon sugar
¼ teaspoon cinnamon

Mix ingredients together and cook as you would other pancakes. Use a non-stick pan with a little olive oil. Flip them when the underside is brown – don't wait for bubbles.

Serve with marmalade sauce (recipe in this book), berry sauce (recipe in this book), sugar free syrup or fresh fruit.

Yield: 4 servings   Serving Size: ¼ cup batter
Per Serving: Calories: 252; Fat: 22.9 g; Carbs: 6.7 g; Dietary Fiber: 3.1 g; Sugar: 1.2 g; Protein: 8.8 g

⚠ The caution sign identifies recipes that include caution items as ingredients. Some high fat caution items are milk, cheese, and nuts. Some high sugar (even though natural sugar) are pineapple and banana. Some high starchy vegetables are black beans and other legumes. These items are caution items for the 1st 3 weeks of maintenance. **Use these recipes in moderation and watch your morning weight closely, particularly during the 1st 3 weeks.**

Bacon & Egg "Hash Browns"

3 cups chopped cauliflower
1 tablespoon olive oil
2 eggs
¼ cup Hormel Real Bacon Bits
½ cup cheddar cheese
Salt and pepper to taste

In a skillet, sauté cauliflower and olive oil for about 10 minutes until cauliflower is tender. Push to the side. Add eggs and scramble in center until they are about done. Toss with cauliflower and add bacon and cheese. When cheese is melted, add salt and pepper to taste and serve.

Yield: 4 servings   **Serving Size: ⅔ cup**
Per Serving: Calories: 162; Fat: 11.8 g; Carbs: 4.3 g; Dietary Fiber: 1.9 g; Sugar: 2.0 g; Protein: 10.8 g

---

⚠ The caution sign identifies recipes that include caution items as ingredients. Some high fat caution items are milk, cheese, and nuts. Some high sugar (even though natural sugar) are pineapple and banana. Some high starchy vegetables are black beans and other legumes. These items are caution items for the 1st 3 weeks of maintenance. **Use these recipes in moderation and watch your morning weight closely, particularly during the 1st 3 weeks.**

Scrambled Eggs With Smoked Salmon

Eggs (2 eggs per person)
2 ounces smoked salmon
1 tablespoon cream
1 teaspoon butter
Chives
Optional: Bread Slice, toasted (from this book)

Slice smoked salmon into strips and finely chop chives. Melt butter and cream over medium heat. Grill or toast the bread. Use 2 eggs per person, beat in a bowl, and add to the butter and cream in the pan. Grill or toast the bread. Blend eggs with a spatula for 1-2 minutes, making sure not to overcook – should be quite moist. Season with salt and pepper to taste. Place the salmon on top of the egg, and top with a generous amount of chives.

Optional: Grill or toast a piece of bread and place the eggs, stacked with salmon and chives, over the toasted bread.

Yield: 1 serving
Per Serving: Calories: 284; Fat: 20.2 g; Carbs: 1.1 g; Dietary Fiber: 0.0 g; Sugar: 0.9 g; Protein: 23.8 g

Crustless Crab Quiche

CAUTION: High FAT

4 eggs
1 cup sour cream
1 cup low fat 2% small curd cottage cheese
½ cup grated Parmesan cheese
¼ cup almond flour
Pinch of sea salt
4 drops Tabasco sauce
Pinch nutmeg
8 ounces diced crabmeat
1 ½ cups shredded Swiss or Monterey jack cheese
½ cup diced Vidalia sweet onion

Preheat oven to 350° F. Lightly grease a 10-inch glass pie plate. In food processor, blend the first 8 ingredients. Pour the mixture into a large bowl and stir in the crabmeat, cheese and onion. Pour mixture into the prepared pie plate and bake for 50 - 60 minutes until set in the middle and is puffed and golden brown. Let stand for 10 minutes before slicing.

Yield: 8 serving   **Serving Size: ⅛ pie**
Per Serving: Calories: 272; Fat: 18.1 g; Carbs: 9.5 g; Dietary Fiber: 0.6 g; Sugar: 2.8 g; Protein: 18.4 g

> **Diet Tip:** Fast food can be OK. There are healthy options available almost everywhere these days. Know your nutritional facts or ask for them at the restaurant.

⚠ The caution sign identifies recipes that include caution items as ingredients. Some high fat caution items are milk, cheese, and nuts. Some high sugar (even though natural sugar) are pineapple and banana. Some high starchy vegetables are black beans and other legumes. These items are caution items for the 1st 3 weeks of maintenance. **Use these recipes in moderation and watch your morning weight closely, particularly during the 1st 3 weeks.**

Basic Tofu Scramble

16 ounces firm tofu
1 teaspoon olive or canola oil
2 tablespoons finely chopped onion
2 scallions, white part only, finely chopped
¼ teaspoon soy sauce
Salt and ground black pepper

Add some oil to a big skillet and sauté the onions. Add tofu, scallions, soy sauce, salt and pepper and scramble like you would eggs. Optional: Add mushrooms, spinach, asparagus, Vidalia onions or vegetables of your choice, either with onions or while scrambling, your preference.

Yield: 4 servings   **Serving Size: 4 ounces**
Per Serving: Calories: 94; Fat: 5.9 g; Carbs: 3.0 g; Dietary Fiber: 1.3 g; Sugar: 1.1 g; Protein: 9.5 g

Flax and Cheese Pancakes or Muffins

(Shown with Berry Syrup)

16 ounces low fat 1% cottage cheese
0 calorie sweetener of choice equal to ½ cup sugar
2 tablespoons melted butter
½ cup flax meal
4 large eggs

Cream cottage cheese with blender or hand mixer until smooth. Use spoon to mix remaining ingredients into cottage cheese until well blended.

To prepare as pancakes: Heat non-stick frying pan on medium. Pour small (3 inch diameter) pancakes. Heat until tops start to bubble and edges start to brown. Flip and heat about 2 minutes longer. Serve with Berry Syrup from this book or sugar free maple syrup.

Yield: 4 servings; 12 pancakes   Serving Size: 3 pancakes
Per Serving: Calories: 263; Fat: 16.4 g; Carbs: 10.1g; Dietary Fiber: 4.0g; Sugar: 3.1g; Protein: 23.1g

To prepare as muffins: Preheat oven to 350° F and spray a non-stick muffin tin with cooking spray. Spoon the mixture into the muffin tin and bake for 40 minutes. You may want to rotate the pan after about 15 minutes to help even the baking. Let cool completely before removing from pan. Some great additions for a twist are vanilla, cinnamon, nutmeg, etc.

Yield: 12 servings   Service Size: 1 muffin
Per Serving: Calories: 94; Fat: 5.8; Carbs: 3.7 g; Dietary Fiber: 1.3 g; Sugar: 0.1 g; Protein: 8.2 g

2nd Three Weeks Option: Add ½ cup chopped nuts or unsweetened coconut.

Per Serving: Calories: 125; Fat: 9.1; Carbs: 4.3; Dietary Fiber: 1.8 g; Sugar: 0.0 g; Protein: 8.6 g

⚠ The caution sign identifies recipes that include caution items as ingredients. Some high fat caution items are milk, cheese, and nuts. Some high sugar (even though natural sugar) are pineapple and banana. Some high starchy vegetables are black beans and other legumes. These items are caution items for the 1st 3 weeks of maintenance. **Use these recipes in moderation and watch your morning weight closely, particularly during the 1st 3 weeks.**

Lifestyle Tip: Have a plan for events and ongoing circumstances. For instance, if a muffin cart comes around your office every morning, bring or buy a healthy muffin to substitute so that you don't feel left out.

Crustless Spinach Quiche

CAUTION: High FAT

1 tablespoon olive oil
6 – 8 chopped scallions
1 (10 ounce) package frozen chopped spinach, thawed and drained (8 cups fresh spinach, chopped)
6 beaten eggs
2 ½ cups shredded cheese, Muenster suggested, but your choice (sharp cheddar, Colby, Gouda, etc.)
¼ teaspoon salt
⅛ teaspoon ground black pepper

Preheat oven to 350° F. Lightly grease a 9 inch pie pan. Heat oil in a large skillet over medium-high heat. Add onions and cook, stirring occasionally, until onions are soft. Stir in spinach and continue cooking until excess moisture has evaporated. In a large bowl, combine eggs, cheese, salt and pepper. Add spinach mixture and stir to blend. Scoop into prepared pie pan. Bake in preheated oven until eggs have set, about 30 - 35 minutes. Edge should start to brown and the center will stop bubbling. Let cool for 10 minutes before serving.

Yield: 8 servings   Serving Size: ⅛ pie
Per Serving: Calories: 205; Fat: 15.7 g; Carbs: 2.9 g; Dietary Fiber: 1.1 g; Sugar: 1.1 g; Protein: 13.7 g

Optional: Add 4 ounces lean chopped ham, mushrooms, and/or thin sliced tomatoes on top.

Yield: 8 servings   Serving Size: ⅛ pie
Per Serving: Calories: 233; Fat: 17.0 g; Carbs: 4.4 g; Dietary Fiber: 1.6 g; Sugar: 1.6 g; Protein: 16.7 g

> ⚠ The caution sign identifies recipes that include caution items as ingredients. Some high fat caution items are milk, cheese, and nuts. Some high sugar (even though natural sugar) are pineapple and banana. Some high starchy vegetables are black beans and other legumes. These items are caution items for the 1st 3 weeks of maintenance. **Use these recipes in moderation and watch your morning weight closely, particularly during the 1st 3 weeks.**

Protein Power Yogurt

1 cup low fat 2% cottage cheese
1 cup 0% fat Greek yogurt
0 calorie sweetener of choice equal to ½ cup sugar

Combine cottage cheese, sweetener, and yogurt in blender; blend until smooth. Serve chilled.

Yield: 2 servings   Serving Size: 1 cup
Per Serving: Calories: 168; Fat: 2.2 g; Carbs: 8.8 g; Dietary Fiber: 0.0 g; Sugar: 5.0 g; Protein: 27.5 g

Crustless Bacon and Egg Quiche

1 tablespoon butter
½ small white Vidalia onion, chopped
8 ounces ⅓ less fat softened cream cheese
4 ounces grated Swiss cheese
5 large eggs
1 cup 2 % milk
6 slices bacon, cooked, drained and crumbled

Preheat oven to 425° F. Sauté onion in butter until transparent.   Cover bottom of the pie pan with cream cheese cut into small pieces. Add bacon and onion, and then top with the grated cheese. Mix together milk and eggs. Pour over the top and bake 15 minutes. Reduce heat to 350 and bake another 30 minutes. Cool slightly; serve warm.

Yield: 8 servings   Serving Size: ⅛ pie
Per Serving: Calories: 228; Fat: 17.8 g; Carbs: 3.6 g; Dietary Fiber: 0.1 g; Sugar: 2.9 g; Protein: 12.2 g

---

⚠ The caution sign identifies recipes that include caution items as ingredients. Some high fat caution items are milk, cheese, and nuts. Some high sugar (even though natural sugar) are pineapple and banana. Some high starchy vegetables are black beans and other legumes. These items are caution items for the 1ˢᵗ 3 weeks of maintenance. **Use these recipes in moderation and watch your morning weight closely, particularly during the 1ˢᵗ 3 weeks.**

Pumpkin Custard

1 egg
⅓ cup unsweetened canned pumpkin
⅓ cup low fat 2% cottage cheese
2 tablespoons 2% milk
Dash of cinnamon, allspice, cloves
0 calorie sweetener of choice equal to 2 teaspoons sugar

Preheat oven to 350° F. Combine all ingredients in a blender until smooth. Divide into two custard cups and place in a pan of water. Bake for 25 to 30 minutes.

Yield: 2 servings
Per Serving: Calories: 87; Fat: 3.3; Carbs: 6.1 g; Dietary Fiber: 1.2 g; Sugar: 2.4 g; Protein: 8.9 g

Healthy Tip: Use a probiotic/digestive enzyme (preferably plant based) daily.

Mexican Quiche

1 tablespoon olive oil
½ red pepper
½ green pepper
3 tablespoons chopped onion
1 pound sirloin tip
¼ cup water
1 packet taco seasoning mix
4 ounces grated pepper jack cheese
1 ½ cups fat free half and half
4 eggs
1 teaspoon salt
Pepper to taste

Preheat oven to 375° F. Sauté peppers and onion in olive oil and set aside. Cut sirloin into bite size pieces and sauté in water and taco seasoning. After meat is cooked*, stir in sautéed vegetables and spread in bottom of pie plate. Sprinkle cheese on top of meat mixture. Combine half and half, eggs, salt and pepper. Beat well and pour over meat and cheese. Bake for 35-40 minutes.

*If meat mixture contains too much liquid, remove meat and cook sauce down before adding vegetables.

Yield: 8 servings   Serving Size: ⅛ pie
Per Serving: Calories: 254; Fat: 12 g; Carbs: 9.3 g; Dietary Fiber: 0.4 g; Sugar: 3.8 g; Protein: 23.7 g

> ⚠ The caution sign identifies recipes that include caution items as ingredients. Some high fat caution items are milk, cheese, and nuts. Some high sugar (even though natural sugar) are pineapple and banana. Some high starchy vegetables are black beans and other legumes. These items are caution items for the 1st 3 weeks of maintenance. **Use these recipes in moderation and watch your morning weight closely, particularly during the 1st 3 weeks.**

Cottage Cheese Fluff

1 cup low fat 2% cottage cheese
¾ cup Cool Whip
½ can (8 ounces) pineapple tidbits, drained
½ package (1 ounce) sugar free strawberry flavored gelatin mix

Combine cottage cheese, pineapple and gelatin. Beat until blended, and then fold in whipped cream. Chill for at least 10 minutes before serving.

Yield: 6 servings   Serving Size: ½ cup
Per Serving: Calories: 94; Fat: 3.1 g; Carbs: 9.2 g; Dietary Fiber: 0.3 g; Sugar: 7.3 g; Protein: 6.6 g

Cottage Cheese Crepes

1 cup low fat 2% small curd cottage cheese
4 eggs
¼ cup almond flour
2 tablespoons melted butter
Cinnamon
Sea salt to taste
Milk to thin (optional)

Blend cottage cheese and 2 eggs for 30 seconds. Scrape the sides of the blender. Add flour and 2 more eggs; blend for another 30 seconds or until pretty smooth. Add cinnamon and salt to taste. If batter is too thick and thinner is preferred, blend in milk. Place 3 tablespoons batter in a sprayed or well-buttered non-stick frying pan and swirl to coat pan. Cook at medium heat until top looks dry. Flip and cook for a few more seconds. Place on a plate and fill with your choice of fresh berries.

Yield: 4 servings   Serving Size: 2 crepes
Per Serving: Calories: 205; Fat: 14.7g; Carbs: 3.9 g; Dietary Fiber: 0.8 g; Sugar: 0.8 g; Protein: 14.9 g

Ricotta & Strawberry Filled Flourless Crepes

Crepes:
2 large eggs
2 tablespoons heavy cream
1 teaspoon olive oil
0 calorie sweetener of choice equal to 2 teaspoons sugar
¼ teaspoon vanilla
⅛ teaspoon cinnamon

Mix well. Use spray on non-stick skillet. Lift skillet off the heat and make each crepe by pouring in 2 tablespoons batter while tilting the pan in all directions to swirl the batter in a thin even layer. Cook on medium until top looks dry and flip for a few seconds. Add 2 tablespoons filling and roll.

Ricotta Filling:
4 strawberries, sliced or smashed
⅓ cup ricotta cheese
0 calorie sweetener of choice equal to 2 teaspoons sugar

Yield: 2 servings   Serving Size: 2 crepes
Per Serving: Calories: 164; Fat: 11.3 g; Carbs: 5.5 g; Dietary Fiber: 0.6 g; Sugar: 1.6 g; Protein: 11.0 g

⚠ The caution sign identifies recipes that include caution items as ingredients. Some high fat caution items are milk, cheese, and nuts. Some high sugar (even though natural sugar) are pineapple and banana. Some high starchy vegetables are black beans and other legumes. These items are caution items for the 1st 3 weeks of maintenance. **Use these recipes in moderation and watch your morning weight closely, particularly during the 1st 3 weeks.**

Cheesecake Pancakes with Fruit

2 cups strawberries, chopped into quarters
½ teaspoon balsamic vinegar
0 calorie sweetener of choice equal to 1 teaspoon sugar
3 eggs, yolks and whites separated
0 calorie sweetener of choice equal to 2 tablespoons sugar
1 teaspoon vanilla
1 cup 4% milk fat cottage cheese
⅓ cup almond flour

Put the strawberries into a bowl and sprinkle with balsamic vinegar and 1 teaspoon 0 calorie sweetener of choice. Stir before covering with plastic wrap and leaving to steep while you make the cheese-cakelets. Mix the egg yolks with the 2 tablespoons 0 calorie sweetener of choice, beating well. Add the vanilla, cottage cheese, and flour. Then, in another bowl, whisk the whites until frothy with a hand whisk and fold into the cottage cheese mixture. Heat a smooth griddle or non-stick skillet and dollop the batter onto it, making pancakes of about 3 to 4 inches in diameter. Each pancake will take a minute or so to firm up underneath. Then you should flip it and cook the other side. Remove to a warmed plate when ready. Turn the strawberries in the ruby syrup they have made and squish some pieces with a fork at the same time. Serve with the hot pancakes.

Yield: 4 servings   Serving Size: 2 pancakes, ¼ cup strawberry syrup mixture
Per Serving: Calories: 187; Fat: 10.7 g; Carbs: 11.3 g; Dietary Fiber: 2.4 g; Sugar: 6.2 g; Protein: 13.6 g

Pineapple Custard

2 eggs
⅔ cup low fat 2% cottage cheese
¾ cup crushed pineapple, drained
0 calorie sweetener equal to 4 teaspoons sugar
Cinnamon to garnish

Preheat oven to 350° F. Blend cottage cheese in blender until smooth. Beat egg until foamy. Blend in cottage cheese, pineapple and sweetener. Split into 2 custard cups. Sprinkle cinnamon on top, place custard cups in a pan of water, and bake for 20 minutes.

Yield: 2 servings   Serving Size: ¾ cup
Per Serving: Calories: 183; Fat: 5.8 g; Carbs: 16.8 g; Dietary Fiber: 0.8 g; Sugar: 11.8 g; Protein: 15.9 g

Artichoke Scramble

4 medium-large artichokes
8 medium egg whites
2 teaspoons minced shallots
1 teaspoon lemon juice
2 to 3 sprigs parsley, minced, for garnish
Salt to taste

Preheat the oven to 425° F. Cut out the hearts from the artichokes and place them on a lightly greased baking sheet. Cook in the oven for 10 to 15 minutes or until soft and done. Coat a medium sauté pan with non-stick cooking spray, then add the shallots and a dash of salt. Lightly sweat the shallots, add the egg whites to the pan and scramble together. Remove from the heat and add the lemon juice. Place the eggs on top of the artichoke hearts. Serve garnished with minced parsley if desired.

Yield: 4 servings   Serving Size: 1 artichoke heart with proportionate eggs
Per Serving: Calories: 109 Fat: 0.4 g; Carbs: 17.9 g; Dietary Fiber: 8.8 g; Sugar: 2.1g; Protein: 12.5 g

Super High Protein Chocolate Yogurt

6 ounces 0% fat Greek yogurt
½ scoop chocolate protein powder
0 calorie sweetener of choice to taste

Mix and serve.

Yield: 1 serving
Per Serving: Calories: 160; Fat: 1.0 g; Carbs: 10.0 g; Dietary Fiber: 0.0 g; Sugar: 8.5 g; Protein: 28.5 g

Shopping Tip: For a quick topping, some reviews suggest sugar free fruit preserves from Natures Hollow: www.natureshollow.com.

Carbalose Flour

Carbalose is touted as revolutionary new flour that can be used in place of wheat flour, but contains 80% less carbs. This may be used similarly to regular flour in most recipes, but from research, slight adjustments to liquids and salt may be necessary. With the help of the internet and the significant reduction of carbs, Carbalose and Quickcarb may be worth your effort. Carbalose has a mere 19 grams of "net carbs" per 100 grams (approximately 1 cup).

Quick noted adjustments: Water or liquids may need slight adjustments. If using yeast or other leavening products, double the amount of leavening products used in the original flour recipe. Drop baking temperature by 25 ° F and slightly increase baking time.

Suggested substitution for your regular (not low carb version) cookbook recipes:
- For straight substitution, start out using ⅔ cup Carbalose per 1 cup of flour in original recipe
- ½ Carbalose and ½ almond flour/meal; can also be used in conjunction with flax meal and coconut flour. These tend to bake faster and need slightly more liquid.
- Learning about resistant wheat starch can also be helpful when using Carbalose for baking. Suggested use is 3 parts Carbalose to 1 part resistant wheat starch (RWS) i.e. ¾ cup Carbalose with ¼ cup resistant wheat starch/almond flour/flax meal.
- Carbalose has salt, so if salt is in a recipe, it should be cut down.
- Double leavening agents i.e. baking powder/soda, when called for in a recipe, and increase liquids slightly.

Many users of Carbalose report great success with pie crusts, hot dog buns, hamburger buns, biscuits, monkey bread, schnitzel, muffins, pizza dough, tarts, fried chicken, garlic bread, French toast, waffles, etc. If you learn the tricks, it is worth the effort.

Carbalose Crepes

2 eggs
1 egg yolk
Dash teaspoon sea salt
½ cup Carbalose flour
¼ cup heavy cream
¼ cup water
1 ½ teaspoons melted butter

Combine eggs, yolks and salt. Gradually whisk in flour, alternately with cream and water, until smooth. Whisk in butter. Chill batter at least 1 hour. Heat medium non-stick skillet to medium heat and spray lightly with cooking spray. Lift skillet off the heat and make each crepe by pouring in 2 tablespoons batter while tilting the pan in all directions to swirl the batter in a thin even layer. Cook until bottom of crepe is browned; flip and brown the other side for a few seconds. Use as crepes or tortillas and fill with fillings in this recipe book or as desired. Store crepes with waxed paper between each one and place in a plastic bag in the refrigerator.

Yield: 6 servings   **Serving Size: 2 crepes**
Per Serving: Calories: 70; Fat: 4.3 g; Carbs: 4.5 g; Dietary Fiber: 0.0 g; Sugar: 0.3 g; Protein: 5.0 g

Breads & Crusts

Banana Bread

1 tablespoon egg substitute
2 ounces light sour cream
½ teaspoon salt
5 medium bananas
¾ cup whole flax seed meal
1 teaspoon baking soda
0 calorie sweetener of choice equal to ¾ cup sugar
¼ cup skim milk

Preheat oven to 350° F. Mix together the sweetener, flaxseed, mashed bananas, milk, sour cream and egg substitute until well blended. Combine the baking soda and salt in a separate bowl. Stir the dry mixture slowly into the banana mixture until moistened (be careful not to over mix). Pour onto a greased cookie sheet. Bake for 30 to 40 minutes until a toothpick inserted in the center comes out clean.

Yield: 12 servings   Serving Size: 1/12 cookie sheet
Per Serving: Calories: 82; Fat: 3.0 g; Carbs: 15.2 g; Dietary Fiber: 3.3 g; Sugar: 6.3 g; Protein: 2.5 g

Pizza Crust/Cheese Bread – Cauliflower Based

2 cups cauliflower
2 eggs
2 cups mozzarella cheese
1 teaspoon onion powder
2 teaspoons oregano
1 teaspoon basil
1 tablespoon Parmesan cheese

Preheat oven to 450° F. Rinse cauliflower, then grate or cut finely. Put in microwaveable dish and cook 4-5 minutes – do not add water. Squeeze out any excess water with a towel. Mix with all other ingredients. Sprinkle a greased cookie sheet with Parmesan cheese, like flouring a pan. Spread mixture evenly, taking care not to let middle of crust get too thick, and bake for 12-15 minutes.

Yield: 8 servings   Serving Size: ⅛ cookie sheet
Per Serving: Calories: 112; Fat: 7.0 g; Carbs: 3.0 g; Dietary Fiber: 0.8 g; Sugar: 1.0 g; Protein: 9.5 g

Blueberry Nut Bread

CAUTION:
High FAT

2 cups whole blueberries (or cranberries or raspberries), fresh or frozen

2 ½ cups almond flour

⅓ cup powdered egg white, i.e. Deb El Just Whites, Honeyville, Bioplex Simply Whites

2 ½ teaspoons baking powder

¾ teaspoon salt

0 calorie sweetener of choice equal to 1 cup sugar

½ cup melted butter (1 stick)

3 eggs

¾ cup water

Preheat oven to 350° F. Butter the bottom and lower part of sides of a large loaf pan. To ensure easy removal, put a piece of parchment paper in the bottom and then butter that as well. Roughly chop the blueberries or pulse in a food processor. Don't chop berries too fine as they shrink during cooking. Mix dry ingredients together.   Add the wet ingredients. Mix well. Pour batter into pan and bake about 40–50 minutes until top is golden brown and toothpick comes out clean.

Yield: 16 servings   Serving Size: 1/16 loaf pan
Per Serving: Calories: 185; Fat: 15.4 g; Carbs: 8.3 g; Dietary Fiber: 2.3 g; Sugar: 2.5 g; Protein: 7.7 g

2nd Three Weeks Option: Add ½ cup chopped pecans or walnuts.

Yield: 16 servings   Serving Size: 1/16 loaf pan
Per Serving: Calories: 208; Fat: 17.8 g; Carbs: 8.8 g; Dietary Fiber: 2.7 g; Sugar: 2.6 g; Protein: 8.0 g

---

⚠ The caution sign identifies recipes that include caution items as ingredients. Some high fat caution items are milk, cheese, and nuts. Some high sugar (even though natural sugar) are pineapple and banana. Some high starchy vegetables are black beans and other legumes. These items are caution items for the 1st 3 weeks of maintenance. **Use these recipes in moderation and watch your morning weight closely, particularly during the 1st 3 weeks.**

Cooking Tip: When interpreting the conversion information on product labels, be sure to read the wording carefully. For example, " ⅓ cup pasteurized egg white equals 2 eggs" is telling you that ⅓ cup of the product equals the equivalent of 2 <u>whole eggs</u>, rather than 2 egg whites.

Pizza Crust – Egg/Cheese Based

6 eggs
6 ounces ⅓ less fat cream cheese
1 teaspoon garlic powder
1½ teaspoons oregano or other Italian seasoning
½ teaspoon salt
¼ teaspoon black pepper
1 cup shredded pizza cheese blend (ex. Parmesan, Romano, Asiago)

Preheat oven to 350° F. Blend egg and cream cheese (at room temperature) with electric mixer. Add salt and spices and mix well. Spread the cup of shredded pizza cheese in the bottom of a pizza pan that has been sprayed with no stick olive oil cooking spray. Pour egg/cream cheese mixture over the shredded cheese and bake for 22-25 minutes until the top begins to brown. Remove from oven, add pizza toppings and bake about another 10-15 minutes until done.

Yield: 8 servings   Serving Size: ⅛ pizza pan
Per Serving: Calories: 137; Fat: 9.1 g; Carbs: 6.5 g; Dietary Fiber: 0.4 g; Sugar: 1.6 g; Protein: 6.5 g

> **Diet Tip:**
> Eat plenty of fiber.

Pizza Crust – Zucchini Based

2 cups shredded (and peeled – optional) zucchini
2 eggs
2 cups shredded mozzarella cheese
1 tablespoon Parmesan cheese

Preheat oven to 450° F. Shred a large zucchini. Squeeze out any excess water with a towel. Mix with all other ingredients except the Parmesan. Sprinkle a greased pizza pan or baking stone with Parmesan cheese, like flouring a pan. Spread 2 cups shredded (and peeled - optional) zucchini mixture evenly, taking care not to let middle of crust get too thick. Bake for 12-15 minutes. Add toppings and bake another 15 minutes until done.

Yield: 8 servings   Serving Size: ⅛ pizza pan
Per Serving: Calories: 108; Fat: 7.0 g; Carbs: 2.1 g; Dietary Fiber: 0.3 g; Sugar: 0.8 g; Protein: 9.3 g

Flax Seed Flat Bread

2 cups golden flax seed meal
1 tablespoon baking powder
1 teaspoon salt
0 calorie sweetener equal to ½ tablespoon sugar
5 beaten eggs
½ cup water
⅓ cup olive oil

Preheat oven to 350° F. Whisk dry ingredients. Combine wet and dry ingredients, mixing well. Make sure there aren't strings of egg white hanging out in the batter. Let batter stand 2 – 3 (no more) minutes to thicken. Pour batter onto a pizza pan or jelly roll pan that is lined with oiled parchment paper. Start in the center and spread outward toward the edges of the pan. Bake for approximately 20 minutes until bread springs back when you touch the top and/or is visibly browned. Bake, cut and serve. This flatbread can be used as a pizza crust or cut in squares and then sliced horizontally to be used as bread.

Yield: 8 servings   Serving Size: ⅛ pizza pan
Per Serving: Calories: 241; Fat: 20.7 g; Carbs: 9.4 g; Dietary Fiber: 8.0 g; Sugar: 0.2 g; Protein: 9.5 g

Pizza Crust – Flax Based

1 ½ cups flax seed meal
2 teaspoons baking powder
1 teaspoon salt
1 teaspoon oregano
0 calorie sweetener equal to 1 tablespoon sugar
3 tablespoons olive oil
3 eggs
½ cup water

Preheat oven to 425° F. Mix dry ingredients together. Add wet ingredients and mix well. Let stand for 5 minutes to thicken. Spread on pizza pan. Bake 15-18 minutes. Top with sauce, cheese, vegetables and meat and bake until cheese is melted.

Yield: 8 servings   Serving Size: ⅛ pizza pan
Per Serving: Calories: 160; Fat: 13.5 g; Carbs: 7.0 g; Dietary Fiber: 6.1 g; Sugar: 0.1 g; Protein: 6.6 g

---

⚠ The caution sign identifies recipes that include caution items as ingredients. Some high fat caution items are milk, cheese, and nuts. Some high sugar (even though natural sugar) are pineapple and banana. Some high starchy vegetables are black beans and other legumes. These items are caution items for the 1st 3 weeks of maintenance. **Use these recipes in moderation and watch your morning weight closely, particularly during the 1st 3 weeks.**

Raspberry Nut Bread

CAUTION: High FAT

2 cups whole raspberries, fresh or frozen, roughly chopped
2 ½ cups almond flour
⅓ cup powdered egg white, i.e. Deb El Just Whites, Honeyville,
   Bioplex Simply Whites
2 ½ teaspoons baking powder
¾ teaspoon salt
0 calorie sweetener equal to 1 cup sugar
½ cup melted butter
3 eggs
¾ cup water
½ cup pecans or walnuts, chopped (optional and included in nutritional information)

Preheat oven to 350° F. Spray a large loaf pan with non-stick cooking spray. To ensure easy removal, put a piece of parchment paper in the bottom and spray that as well.   Mix dry ingredients together. Add the wet ingredients. Mix well. Pour batter into pan and bake about 40–50 minutes until top is golden brown and toothpick comes out clean.

Yield: 12 servings   Serving Size: 1/12 loaf pan
Per Serving: Calories: 206; Fat: 16.1 g; Carbs: 10.6 g; Dietary Fiber: 4.3 g; Sugar: 2.0 g; Protein: 10.7 g

Peanut Pie Crust

CAUTION: High FAT

(Shown with Peanut Butter Pie)

¾ cup crushed peanuts or ¾ cup almond meal
¼ cup finely chopped pecans
2 tablespoons melted butter
0 calorie sweetener equal to 2 tablespoons sugar

Preheat oven to 350° F. Combine ingredients for crust and press into bottom and sides of a 9" pie pan. Bake 7 – 10 minutes until beginning to brown.

Yield: 8 servings   Serving Size: ⅛ pie
Per Serving: Calories: 126; Fat: 12.1 g; Carbs: 3.1 g; Dietary Fiber: 1.5 g; Sugar: 0.7 g; Protein: 3.9 g

⚠ The caution sign identifies recipes that include caution items as ingredients. Some high fat caution items are milk, cheese, and nuts. Some high sugar (even though natural sugar) are pineapple and banana. Some high starchy vegetables are black beans and other legumes. These items are caution items for the 1st 3 weeks of maintenance. **Use these recipes in moderation and watch your morning weight closely, particularly during the 1st 3 weeks.**

Almond Pie Crust

(Shown with Strawberry Pie)

¾ cup almond meal
2 tablespoons butter
0 calorie sweetener equal to 2 tablespoons sugar

Preheat oven to 325° F. Combine ingredients for crust and press into bottom of pan. Bake 7 – 10 minutes until beginning to brown.

Yield: 8 servings   **Serving Size: ⅛ pie**
Per Serving: Calories: 86; Fat: 8.1 g; Carbs: 2.6 g; Dietary Fiber: 1.1 g; Sugar: 0.4 g; Protein: 2.3 g

---

Healthy Tip: Include healthy fats like almonds and coconut oil in your daily plan.

Flax Almond Pie Crust

3 tablespoons flax flour
¾ cup almond flour
¼ teaspoon sea salt
3 tablespoons butter
0 calorie sweetener of choice equal to ⅓ cup sugar

Preheat oven to 375° F. In one bowl, mix together the flax, almond flour and salt. In a separate bowl, melt the butter and stir in the 0 calorie sweetener of choice. Combine both mixtures together thoroughly. Spray a 9" pie pan with non-stick spray. Spread the batter out (may need to use a spatula). Bake approximately 10 – 12 minutes or until the crust is relatively firm and a bit browned. Let cool thoroughly.

Yield: 8 servings   **Serving Size: ⅛ pie**
Per Serving: Calories: 110; Fat: 10.5 g; Carbs: 4.1 g; Dietary Fiber: 1.9 g; Sugar: 0.4 g; Protein: 2.9 g

---

⚠ The caution sign identifies recipes that include caution items as ingredients. Some high fat caution items are milk, cheese, and nuts. Some high sugar (even though natural sugar) are pineapple and banana. Some high starchy vegetables are black beans and other legumes. These items are caution items for the 1ˢᵗ 3 weeks of maintenance. **Use these recipes in moderation and watch your morning weight closely, particularly during the 1ˢᵗ 3 weeks.**

Appetizers

Artichoke Cheese Squares

2 tablespoons olive oil
3 finely chopped green onions
1 crushed garlic clove
2 jars (6 oz.) drained, rinsed and chopped artichoke hearts
½ teaspoon oregano
⅛ teaspoon crushed red pepper flakes
4 large beaten eggs
1 cup shredded Monterey jack or pepper jack cheese
2 tablespoons flax seed meal
2 tablespoons parsley
½ teaspoon salt
¼ teaspoon pepper

Preheat oven to 325° F. Heat oil and sauté green onion over medium-high heat until soft, about 4 minutes. Add garlic and continue to sauté for 30 seconds. Add artichokes, oregano and pepper flakes and sauté for about 2 minutes longer until artichokes are warmed through. Set aside to cool for 5 minutes. In a mixing bowl, whisk eggs gently with cheese, flax seed meal, parsley, salt and pepper. Using a wooden spoon, stir in sautéed mixture. Pour batter into an 8 in. square baking dish sprayed with non-stick cooking spray. Bake 30 minutes until golden on top. Cool 10 minutes and cut into squares.

Yield: 4 servings   Serving Size: ¼ pie pan
Per Serving: Calories: 265; Fat: 22.9 g; Carbs: 8.6 g; Dietary Fiber: 4.4 g; Sugar: 0.5 g; Protein: 10.9 g

Yogurt Vegetable Dip

1 package onion soup mix
12 ounces 2% Greek Yogurt

Blend and serve with fresh vegetables of choice.

Yield: 8 servings   Serving Size: 3 tablespoons
Per Serving: Calories: 37; Fat: 0.9 g; Carbs: 3.9 g; Dietary Fiber: 0.2 g; Sugar: 1.9 g; Protein: 3.8 g

Pizza Sauce Dip

1 (14.5 ounce) can Hunt's fire roasted tomatoes
3 tablespoons tomato paste
¼ cup roasted peppers
¼ teaspoon salt
¼ teaspoon oregano
½ teaspoon garlic powder

Combine ingredients and mix well.   Great served with
Cauliflower or Zucchini Crust/Bread.

Yield: 8 servings   Serving Size: ¼ cup
Per Serving: Calories: 22; Fat: 0.0 g; Carb: 4.6 g; Dietary Fiber: 0.7 g; Sugar: 2.5 g; Protein: 0.9 g

Guacamole

3 ripe avocados, peeled
2 tablespoons lime juice
½ teaspoon sea salt
½ teaspoon ground cumin
¼ teaspoon chili powder
½ medium diced onion
2 ripe tomatoes, seeded and finely chopped
1 tablespoon chopped cilantro
1 clove minced garlic

Toss the avocados with the lime juice to coat and avoid browning of the avocados. Drain, reserving the lime juice. Using a potato masher or mixer, combine the avocados, salt, cumin, and chili powder. Fold in the onions, tomatoes, cilantro, and garlic. Add back 1 tablespoon of the reserved lime juice. Let stand at room temperature for 1 hour before serving.

Yield: 10 servings   Serving Size: ⅓ cup
Per Serving: Calories: 104; Fat: 8.9 g; Carbs: 6.9 g; Dietary Fiber: 4.4 g; Sugar: 1.3 g; Protein: 1.5 g

Healthkick Guacomole (Spirulina)

2 tablespoons lime juice
2 cloves garlic
3 tablespoons spirulina (Earthrise brand has good reviews.)
2 avocados
1 tomato
2 tablespoons chili sauce
½ medium onion
Salt and pepper to taste
0 calorie sweetener of choice equal to 2 teaspoons sugar (Optional)

Blend all ingredients.

Yield: 4 servings   Serving Size: ⅓ cup
Per Serving: Calories: 198; Fat: 15.5 g; Carbs: 16.9 g; Dietary Fiber: 7.2 g; Sugar: 3.8 g; Protein: 5.4 g

Italian Cheese Skewers

8 ounces mozzarella cheese
8 ounces cherry tomatoes
8 ounce bottle Zesty Italian Dressing
Dried Basil (in spice isle)
Entertaining skewers

Cut the mozzarella cheese into one inch cubes. Alternate 2 cheese cubes and 2 tomatoes on skewer. Place in a pan and drench with the dressing. Let marinate for at least 2 hours. This should not be refrigerated. Cheese is meant to be served at room temperature. Place on a plate, sprinkle with dried basil, and serve.

Yield: 8 servings   Serving Size: 1 skewer
Per Serving: Calories: 173; Fat: 13.8 g; Carbs: 5.2 g; Dietary Fiber: 0.3 g; Sugar: 3.3 g; Protein: 7.7 g

---

⚠ The caution sign identifies recipes that include caution items as ingredients. Some high fat caution items are milk, cheese, and nuts. Some high sugar (even though natural sugar) are pineapple and banana. Some high starchy vegetables are black beans and other legumes. These items are caution items for the 1st 3 weeks of maintenance. **Use these recipes in moderation and watch your morning weight closely, particularly during the 1st 3 weeks.**

Spinach-Artichoke Dip

2 cups Parmesan cheese
⅔ cup low fat sour cream
1 cup ⅓ less fat cream cheese, softened
2 tablespoons minced garlic
1 (14 ounce) can chopped artichokes
1 frozen box spinach, thawed and drained

Preheat oven to 375° F. Mix all ingredients.
Bake for 25-30 minutes. This dip serves well with Low
Carb Flax Bread recipe in this book.

Yield: 16 servings   Serving Size: ⅓ cup
Per Serving: Calories: 120; Fat: 7.6 g; Carb: 5.0 g; Dietary Fiber: 1.8 g; Sugar: 1.3 g; Protein: 7.5 g

Bruschetta Dip

1(8 ounce) package ⅓ less fat cream cheese, softened
3 ripe tomatoes, chopped
3 tablespoons Zesty Italian dressing
4 tablespoons shredded Parmesan cheese
1 tablespoon finely chopped basil

Spread cream cheese onto bottom of 9 inch pie plate. Mix tomatoes and dressing; spoon over cream cheese. Sprinkle with Parmesan cheese and basil. Serve with assorted cut up vegetables.

Yield: 12 servings   Serving Size: 2 tablespoons
Per Serving: Calories: 85; Fat: 6.8 g; Carb: 2.8 g; Dietary Fiber: 0.4 g; Sugar: 2.2 g; Protein: 2.7 g

> *Tasty Tip:* After the 1st 3 weeks, try this Bruschetta Dip with wheat thins.

Steak Dip

1 cup light mayonnaise
⅛ cup mustard
2 tablespoons A1 sauce
1 tablespoon Durkee Grill Creations Kansas City Style
    Steak Seasoning

Mix together and serve with steak and chicken skewers.
Also makes a great marinade.

Yield: 10 servings   Serving Size: 2 tablespoons
Per Serving: Calories: 85; Fat: 7.9 g; Carb: 2.6 g; Dietary Fiber: 0.3 g; Sugar: 0.5 g; Protein: 0.7 g

Buffalo Chicken Dip

2 large (6 ounce) boneless chicken breasts
6 tablespoons hot sauce
1 (8 ounce) package cream cheese
½ cup Ranch or Blue Cheese dressing
½ cup shredded cheddar cheese

Put chicken in skillet. Add enough water to cover. Bring to a boil over high heat. Reduce heat to medium, cover and poach for 6-7 minutes or until done. Cool, and then shred using 2 forks. Place chicken and hot sauce in a medium skillet. Heat; add cream cheese and dressing until well blended. Add half the shredded cheese and stir until melted. Place in a crock pot and sprinkle top with remaining cheese. Serve warm.

Yield: 12 servings   Serving Size: ¼ cup
Per Serving: Calories: 159; Fat: 11.7 g; Carb: 1.3 g; Dietary Fiber: 0.1 g; Sugar: 1.2 g; Protein: 10.9 g

Hot Taco Dip

1 pound lean ground beef
1 package taco seasoning
1 (15 ounce) can black beans
16 ounces low fat sour cream
2 cups shredded cheddar cheese

Preheat oven to 350° F. Brown meat and drain. Add taco seasoning to meat and cook as directed on package. Place meat in 9 x 13 dish. Add refried beans on top of meat. Spread sour cream over beans and top with shredded cheese. Place in 350 degree oven and bake for 30 minutes or until cheese starts bubbling. Serve with celery or alone immediately.

Yield: 12 servings   Serving Size: ½ cup
Per Serving: Calories: 233; Fat: 12.4 g; Carb: 6.9 g; Dietary Fiber: 1.6 g; Sugar: 1.4 g; Protein: 19.7 g

---

⚠ The caution sign identifies recipes that include caution items as ingredients. Some high fat caution items are milk, cheese, and nuts. Some high sugar (even though natural sugar) are pineapple and banana. Some high starchy vegetables are black beans and other legumes. These items are caution items for the 1st 3 weeks of maintenance. **Use these recipes in moderation and watch your morning weight closely, particularly during the 1st 3 weeks.**

Pickle Rolls

8 Clausen Dill Pickle Wedges
8 slices of deli ham, sliced a little thick, not shaved
4 tablespoons cream cheese, softened

Take a piece of ham, spread ½ tablespoon cream cheese on ham, place the pickle on the ham and cream cheese and roll.

Yield: 8 servings   Serving Size: 1 pickle roll
Per Serving: Calories: 65; Fat: 4.2 g; Carb: 1.6 g; Dietary Fiber: 0.6 g; Sugar: 0.2 g; Protein: 5.1 g

> *Diet Tip:* Switch from whole milk to 2% or skim milk for some of your dairy uses.

Stuffed Mushrooms

1 pound large fresh white mushrooms
1 tablespoon olive oil
6 ounces sausage
½ cup chopped green onions
1 teaspoon chopped garlic
½ teaspoon Italian seasoning
½ cup shredded mozzarella cheese
¼ cup grated Parmesan cheese

Preheat oven to 400° F. Rinse mushrooms and remove stems. Finely chop the stems to equal ½ cup and set them aside. Toss mushroom caps with 1 tablespoon olive oil and place in a shallow baking pan.   Place sausage, green onion, garlic, Italian seasoning and reserved chopped mushroom stems in a skillet on high heat. Sauté for about 5 minutes until browned. Drain any excess grease and add both cheeses, stirring until cheese melts. Scoop sausage mixture into mushroom caps and bake for 10-15 minutes until mushrooms are tender.

Yield: 12 servings   Serving Size: approximately 2 caps
Per Serving: Calories: 112; Fat: 8.2 g; Carb: 2.2 g; Dietary Fiber: 0.5 g; Sugar 0.8 g; Protein: 7.7 g

Meatballs

1 pound lean ground beef
3 egg whites
¼ cup Parmesan cheese
1 teaspoon oregano
1 teaspoon garlic powder
1 tablespoon onion powder
1 ½ teaspoons salt
½ teaspoon pepper

Combine all ingredients and mix well. Roll into 12 meat balls and fry in pan until all sides are browned. For an entrée, serve with miracle noodles and spaghetti sauce.

Yield: 4 servings   Serving Size: 3 meatballs
Per Serving: Calories: 260; Fat: 8.9 g; Carb: 2.8 g; Dietary Fiber: 0.4 g; Sugar 1.0 g; Protein: 39.9 g

Fiesta Dip

8 ounce package ⅓ less fat cream cheese
2 tablespoons cream
3 tablespoons sugar free French dressing (store bought or from recipe in this book)
⅓ cup Heinz Low Carb Ketchup or from recipe in this book
1 ½ tablespoons grated sweet onion
½ teaspoon sea salt
Hot sauce to taste

Blend all ingredients until smooth. Serve with raw vegetables of your choice i.e. carrots, broccoli, celery, peppers, grape tomatoes, etc.

Yield: 8 servings   Serving Size: 2 tablespoons
Per Serving: Calories: 56.8; Fat: 2.5 g; Carb: 4.6 g; Dietary Fiber: 0.1 g; Sugar: 2.2 g; Protein: 4.2 g

Cucumber Sandwiches

1 package ⅓ less fat cream cheese
1 dry packet Zesty Italian dressing mix
2 large cucumbers

Garnishment:
Fresh dill
1 pint sliced cherry tomatoes

Mix cream cheese and dressing mix. Cut each cucumber into approximately 24 (⅓") slices and spread with cream cheese mixture. Garnish with cherry tomatoes and dill.

Yield: 8 servings   Serving Size: approximately 6 slices
Per Serving: Calories: 104; Fat: 6.4 g; Carb: 8.5 g; Dietary Fiber: 0.8 g; Sugar: 3.3 g; Protein: 3.0 g

Deviled Eggs

6 hard-boiled eggs, peeled and cut lengthwise
⅓ cup mayonnaise
2 tablespoons sweet pickle relish
½ teaspoon dry ground mustard
½ teaspoon white vinegar
⅛ teaspoon sea salt
¼ teaspoon ground black pepper
 Paprika for garnish

Pop out the egg yolks to a small bowl and mash with a fork. Add mayonnaise, sweet relish, mustard powder, vinegar, salt and pepper and mix thoroughly. Scoop the mixture into the empty egg white shells and sprinkle lightly with paprika. Store covered lightly with plastic wrap and serve within one day for optimum flavor and consistency. Optional: 2-3 dashes of your favorite hot sauce

Yield: 6 servings   Serving Size: 2 egg halves
Per Serving: Calories: 122; Fat: 8.8 g; Carb: 5.4 g; Dietary Fiber: 0.1 g; Sugar: 2.7 g; Protein: 5.8 g

Chili Dip

1 (8 ounce) package cream cheese softened
1 (15 ounce) can chili without beans
1 can Rotel tomatoes, drained
¼ teaspoon chili powder

In a medium bowl, mix cream cheese, chili, tomatoes and chili powder. Microwave cream cheese mixture on high for 1 minute. Remove from microwave, stir, and repeat until the mixture is melted and blended.

Yield: 12 servings   Serving Size: ¼ cup
Per Serving: Calories: 87; Fat: 5.5 g; Carb: 4.8 g; Dietary Fiber: 0.9 g; Sugar: 2.1 g; Protein: 4.1 g

> *Lifestyle Tip:* Write down your reason for wanting to get healthy. This helps your subconscious and your conscious reach your goals faster. Hanging up pictures that represent your goals also helps.

Jalapeno Poppers

25 fresh jalapenos
8 ounces ground sausage, cooked and drained
8 ounces cream cheese
8 ounces shredded Parmesan cheese

Preheat oven to 350° F. Spray baking sheet or line it with foil. Slice peppers in half lengthwise removing veins and seeds. Brown sausage on low until it is crumbly; then drain off excess grease. After it cools, mix in cream cheese and Parmesan cheese. Fill peppers with a heaping teaspoon of mixture and place on baking sheet. Bake for approximately 30 minutes until tops are lightly browned. Cool slightly and serve.

Yield: 16 servings   Serving Size: 3 pieces
Per Serving: Calories: 154; Fat: 11.4 g; Carb: 2.7 g; Dietary Fiber: 0.9 g; Sugar 1.4 g; Protein: 9.5 g

Healthy Tip: Switch from eggs to egg whites occasionally.

Crab Meat Deviled Eggs

6 hard-boiled eggs, peeled and cut lengthwise
1 small can (6 ounces) salad crab meat, rinsed and drained well
¼ cup mayonnaise
1½ tablespoons very finely chopped celery
2 teaspoons Dijon mustard
1 teaspoon fresh squeezed lemon
1 tablespoon basil
½ teaspoon onion powder (add a little more to taste if desired)
A few drops of Worcestershire sauce
¼ teaspoon sea salt
¼ teaspoon ground black pepper
Fresh chives, snipped to garnish
Paprika

Remove the egg yolks to a small bowl and mash with a fork. Add mayonnaise, celery, mustard, basil, onion powder, Worcestershire sauce, salt and pepper and mix well. Stir in lemon and crab meat. Spoon the mixture to fill the egg whites and sprinkle lightly with paprika. Serve chilled.

Yield: 6 servings   Serving Size: 2 egg halves
Per Serving: Calories: 129; Fat: 8.2 g; Carb: 3.7 g; Dietary Fiber: 0.1 g; Sugar: 1.1 g; Protein: 9.3 g

Roasted Red Pepper Dip

1 cup mayonnaise
⅓ cup grated raw Parmesan cheese
12 ounces un-marinated artichoke hearts
⅛ teaspoon garlic powder
2 tablespoons chopped red onion
1 cup roasted red peppers

Preheat oven to 350° F. Place all ingredients in food processor and process until smooth. Spray baking dish and transfer dip. Bake for 30 minutes and serve warm.

Yield: 12 servings   Serving Size: ¼ cup
Per Serving: Calories: 106; Fat: 7.4 g; Carb: 8.9 g; Dietary Fiber: 1.7 g; Sugar: 2.3 g; Protein: 2.4 g

European Tomatoes

(Shown with Stuffed Peppers with Tuna)

8 tomato halves
½ cup shredded part-skim mozzarella cheese
2 tablespoons grated Parmesan cheese
1 clove minced garlic
2 tablespoons dried basil
Pinch of sea salt
Dash of pepper

Preheat oven to 400° F. Scrape out inside of tomato halves into a bowl. Chop pulp and combine with all other ingredients. Scoop tomato mixture in tomato halves and place on cookie sheet. Bake for about 10 minutes until cheese is slightly browned and melted. Tomatoes are served warm.

Yield: 8 servings   Serving Size: 1 tomato half
Per Serving: Calories: 39; Fat: 1.9 g; Carb: 2.9 g; Dietary Fiber: 0.8 g; Sugar: 1.7 g; Protein: 2.9 g

Diet Tip: Get a buddy to meet and do activities with you. Play tennis, volleyball, golf or go dancing. Choose activities that you consider a reward instead of a punishment.

Cold Veggie Pizza

Crust:
1 ½ cups flax seed meal
2 teaspoons baking powder
1 teaspoon salt
1 teaspoon oregano
0 calorie sweetener equal to 1 tablespoon sugar
3 tablespoons olive oil
3 eggs
½ cup water

Preheat oven to 425° F. Mix dry ingredients together. Add wet ingredients and mix well. Let set for 5 minutes to thicken. Spread on pizza pan. Bake for 15-18 minutes; let cool.

Topping:
1 (8 ounce) package ⅓ less fat cream cheese, softened to room temperature
1 packet Buttermilk Ranch Dressing mix
1 cup chopped cauliflower
1 cup chopped broccoli
½ cup chopped tomatoes
¼ cup part-skim mozzarella cheese
¼ cup cheddar cheese

Combine cream cheese and salad dressing. Spread on baked, cooled pizza crust. Sprinkle fresh vegetables, then cheese on pizza crust. Cut into 8 slices. Serve cold.

Yield: 8 servings   Serving Size: ⅛ Pizza Pan
Per Serving: Calories: 349; Fat: 27.7 g; Carb: 14.1 g; Dietary Fiber: 8.6 g; Sugar: 2.2 g; Protein: 12.9 g

---

⚠ The caution sign identifies recipes that include caution items as ingredients. Some high fat caution items are milk, cheese, and nuts. Some high sugar (even though natural sugar) are pineapple and banana. Some high starchy vegetables are black beans and other legumes. These items are caution items for the 1st 3 weeks of maintenance. **Use these recipes in moderation and watch your morning weight closely, particularly during the 1st 3 weeks.**

Diet Tip: Keep some healthy frozen and ready-to-eat food on hand. Most of us are pressed for time, so handy, healthy food saves us money and encourages healthy eating.

> **Note:** If a recipe has a significant amount of protein, fat is considered somewhat a given (i.e. eggs and meat are naturally higher in fat than starches, vegetables or natural sugars like fruit) and, therefore, these items are not considered high fat unless 'caution' items such as cheese, nuts, and/or nut flours, i.e. almond flour, are also a part of the recipe.

Pepsi Pot Roast

3 pound pot roast
1 can 98% fat free cream of mushroom soup
1 package dry onion soup mix
1 can diet cola

Place roast in crock pot. Whisk together remaining ingredients and pour over roast. Cover and cook on high 6 hours.

Yield: 12 servings   **Serving Size: 4 ounces**
Per Serving: Calories: 400; Fat: 27.5 g; Carb: 4.0 g; Dietary Fiber: 0.4 g; Sugar: 0.4 g; Protein: 31.8 g

Beef Fajitas

1 pound steak
1 orange pepper
1 yellow pepper
1 green pepper
½ onion – chunked
1 package fajita mix
½ cup water

Cut steak into long strips about ½ inch thick. Slice peppers lengthwise about ½ inch thick. In a non-stick skillet, heat meat and vegetables on medium heat. When the meat is almost done, add seasoning mix and water and sauté until done. Place on top of a plate of lettuce and tomato for a fajita salad.

Yield: 4 servings   **Serving Size: 4 ounces**
Per Serving: Calories: 286; Fat: 5.8 g; Carb: 11.1 g; Dietary Fiber: 1.7 g; Sugar: 2.3 g; Protein: 42.1 g

Fiesta Meat Loaf

1 pound lean ground beef
1 ¼ cups salsa
4 eggs
½ cup coarsely chopped mushrooms

Preheat oven to 350° F. Spray loaf pan with non-stick cooking spray. In a large bowl, combine beef, salsa, eggs, tomatoes and mushrooms. Shape mixture into loaf. Place loaf in pan. Bake until browned, about 1 hour, let stand about 10 minutes before slicing.

Yield: 4 servings   Serving Size: approximately 4 ounces
Per Serving: Calories: 298.0; Fat: 11.6 g; Carb: 5.7 g; Dietary Fiber: 1.4 g; Sugar: 3.0 g; Protein: 41.5 g

2nd Three Weeks Option: Eliminate 2 of the 4 eggs and add ½ cup of oatmeal and a finely grated carrot to the mixture.

Yield: 4 servings   Serving Size: approximately 4 ounces
Per Serving: Calories: 295; Fat: 9.0 g; Carb: 13.9 g; Dietary Fiber: 2.9 g; Sugar: 3.5 g; Protein: 38.8 g

Taiwanese Fried Tofu

1 (8 ounce) package extra firm tofu
3 tablespoons light soy sauce
1 teaspoon balsamic vinegar
½ teaspoon sesame oil
0 calorie sweetener of choice equal to ½ teaspoon sugar
2 tablespoons olive oil
2 cloves garlic, minced
2 tablespoons chopped green onions
Sea salt and ground pepper to taste

Cut the tofu in half lengthwise down the top. Slice into squares ¼ inch thick. Stir together the soy sauce, vinegar, sesame oil, and sweetener in a small bowl, set aside. Heat olive oil in a large, non-stick pan over medium heat. Add garlic and green onions and cook 20-30 seconds. Brown tofu well on each side. Add sauce mixture and cook until the sauce has been mostly absorbed by the tofu (2 to 3 minutes). Season to taste with salt and pepper.

Yield: 2 servings   Serving Size: 4 ounces
Per Serving: Calories: 237; Fat: 19.4 g; Carb: 6.5 g; Dietary Fiber: 1.3 g; Sugar: 3.7 g; Protein: 11 g

Beef Stew

2 pounds stew beef
2 tablespoons olive oil
2 cups water
1 tablespoon Worcestershire sauce
1 clove garlic, peeled
1 medium Vidalia onion, sliced
1 teaspoon sea salt
0 calorie sweetener equal to 1 teaspoon sugar
½ teaspoon fresh ground pepper
½ teaspoon paprika
Dash ground allspice
2 large carrots, sliced
3 stalks celery, chopped
2 diced turnips (optional)
2 tablespoons cornstarch

Heat oil. Brown meat in oil. Add water, Worcestershire sauce, garlic, bay leaves, onion, salt, sweetener, pepper, paprika, and allspice. Cover and simmer 1 ¼ hours. Remove garlic clove. Add carrots, celery and turnips. Cover and cook ¾ to 1 hour longer. To thicken gravy, remove ½ cup hot liquid. Using a separate bowl, combine ¼ cup room temperature water and cornstarch until smooth. Mix with the hot liquid and return mixture to pot. Stir and cook until bubbling.

Yield: 8 servings   Serving Size: 1 cup
Per Serving: Calories: 228; Fat: 10.3 g; Carb: 7.5 g; Dietary Fiber: 1.4 g; Sugar: 3.1 g; Protein: 25.6 g

Mongolian Beef & Bean Sprouts

1 package Sun Bird Mongolian Beef seasoning mix
¼ cup soy sauce
2 tablespoons water
1 pound lean beef
2 teaspoons oil
1 can bean sprouts, drained
2 tablespoons sun dried tomatoes

Combine seasoning packet with soy sauce and water. Set aside. In a skillet, heat oil on high. Slice meat into strips and cook until pink in center. Remove meat. Add soy sauce mixture, tomatoes and drained bean sprouts. Cook until bean sprouts are tender, about 10 minutes, and sauce comes to a boil to thicken. Serve beef on top of bean sprouts.

Yield: 4 servings   Serving Size: 4 ounces
Per Serving: Calories: 301; Fat: 9.9 g; Carb: 12.1 g; Dietary Fiber: 0.3 g; Sugar: 0.9 g; Protein: 40.8 g

Mexican "Rice"

1 pound lean sausage
1 cup salsa
1 chopped green pepper
1 cup chopped onion
3 cups chopped cauliflower
3 slices Monterey Pepper Jack cheese

Brown sausage and drain off grease. Brown onion with sausage.   Add remaining ingredients except cheese. Cook until cauliflower is tender, about 15 minutes. Add cheese and stir until melted.

Yield: 4 servings
Per Serving: Calories: 318; Fat: 15.9 g; Carb: 18.2 g; Dietary Fiber: 3.9 g; Sugar: 5.7 g; Protein: 25.4 g

Pecan Mahi Mahi

¼ cup pecan halves
2 (8 ounce) fresh mahi mahi fillets
½ teaspoon sea salt
¼ teaspoon garlic powder
⅛ teaspoon pepper
2 tablespoons butter
Lemon juice - optional

Lightly process pecans, sea salt, garlic powder, and pepper in a food processor until finely chopped. Press fish in mixture. Melt butter in a large non-stick skillet over medium-high heat; add fish, and cook 3 to 4 minutes on each side or until well browned and fish flakes with a fork. This dish serves nicely with green beans, asparagus or broccoli. Spritz with lemon juice, if desired.

Yield: 3 servings
Per Serving: Calories: 313; Fat: 16.2 g; Carb: 1.5 g; Dietary Fiber: 0.9 g; Sugar: 0.4 g; Protein: 41.5 g

---

⚠ The caution sign identifies recipes that include caution items as ingredients. Some high fat caution items are milk, cheese, and nuts. Some high sugar (even though natural sugar) are pineapple and banana. Some high starchy vegetables are black beans and other legumes. These items are caution items for the 1st 3 weeks of maintenance. **Use these recipes in moderation and watch your morning weight closely, particularly during the 1st 3 weeks.**

Shirataki (Also known as Miracle Noodles and yam noodles)

Shirataki is derived from the Konjac root. Konjac provides Glycomannan which is water soluble dietary fiber. When the fiber is processed as plain shirataki, it has virtually no calories, and is almost 0 net carbs. For some, this provides an acceptable form of pasta. Attention to detail in preparation greatly enhances final outcome.

Two Meat Lasagna

1 ¼ pounds lean ground beef
1 ¼ pounds ground Italian Sausage
1 onion
2 cloves garlic, minced
2 teaspoons ground oregano
1 teaspoon ground basil
¼ teaspoon sea salt
1 (14.5 ounce) can diced tomatoes
2 (15 ounce) cans tomato sauce
1 ½ cups low fat 2% small curd cottage cheese
1 (5 ounce) package grated Parmigiano-Reggiano
2 tablespoons freshly chopped parsley leaves
1 large egg, slightly beaten
1 (6 or 7 ounce) package Shirataki (fiber) Noodles*
2 (8 ounce) packages shredded mozzarella

*For best results when using Shirataki Noodles: Prior to use in a recipe, drain and thoroughly rinse the noodles with cold water. Place drained noodles in a non-stick frying pan and cook over medium heat, stirring occasionally, for approximately 10 minutes.

Preheat oven to 350° F. In a large saucepan, combine ground beef, sausage, onion and garlic. Cook over medium heat until browned and crumbled; drain. Return meat to pan and add oregano, basil, salt and pepper. Add tomatoes, tomato sauce and paste. Bring to a boil, reduce heat and let simmer for 30-45 minutes. In a small bowl, combine cottage cheese, grated cheese, parsley and egg. Spoon ¼ of sauce into bottom of 13 x 9 inch baking pan. Place thin layer of prepared noodles, top with sauce and then cheese. Repeat layers, ending with sauce. Bake for 45 minutes. Top with remaining cheese and bake 15 minutes or until hot and bubbly. Let rest 10 minutes before serving. Divide into 12 pieces.

Yield: 12 servings   Serving Size: 1 piece
Per Serving: Calories: 475; Fat: 28.5 g; Carb: 9.7 g; Dietary Fiber: 1.8 g; Sugar: 4.8 g; Protein: 43.7 g

⚠ The caution sign identifies recipes that include caution items as ingredients. Some high fat caution items are milk, cheese and nuts. Some high starchy vegetables are black beans and other legumes. These items are caution items are milk, cheese, and nuts. Some high sugar (even though natural sugar) are pineapple and bananas for the 1st 3 weeks of maintenance. **Use these recipes in moderation and watch your morning weight closely, particularly during the 1st 3 weeks.**

Caramelized Tofu

8 ounces extra firm tofu, cut to thin 1 inch strips
¼ teaspoon fine grain sea salt
2 teaspoons olives
2 medium cloves garlic, minced
¼ cup pecans, toasted and chopped
0 calorie brown sugar sweetener of your choice equal to 3 tablespoons brown sugar
½ pound Brussels sprouts cut into ⅛ inch wide ribbons

Cook the tofu strips in large hot skillet with ¼ teaspoon salt and a teaspoon of oil. Sauté until slightly golden (3.5 – 5 minutes). Add the garlic and pecans and cook for another minute. Stir in 0 calorie sweetener of your choice. Cook for another couple of minutes. Scrape the tofu out onto a plate and set aside while you cook the Brussels sprouts. In the same pan, add remaining oil, add remaining salt, and turn the heat up to medium-high. When the pan is hot, stir in the strips of Brussels sprouts. Cook for 2 - 3 minutes, stirring a couple times, but not constantly, until you get some golden bits, and the rest of the sprouts are bright and delicious. Combine with tofu mixture and serve.

Yield: 3 servings   Serving Size: approximately 4 ounces
Per Serving: Calories: 168; Fat: 11.3 g; Carb: 11.8 g; Dietary Fiber: 4.1 g; Sugar: 2.4 g; Protein: 11.0 g

Pork Stir-Fry

1 pound pork sirloin
1 bag frozen stir fry vegetables
1 packet stir fry seasoning mix (Sunbird Brand)
2 tablespoons soy sauce
0 calorie sweetener equal to 1 teaspoon sugar
⅓ cup water
2 tablespoons olive oil

In a small bowl, blend soy sauce, sugar, water and seasoning mix. Place oil in a frying pan & saute pork until pink is gone. Add vegetables and sauce mix. Continue to cook until vegetables are tender.

Yield: 6 servings   Serving Size: 1 cup
Per Serving Calories: 245; Fat: 10.9 g; Carb: 12.7 g; Dietary Fiber: 3.4 g; Sugar: 2.5 g; Protein 22.8 g

> *Lifestyle Tip:* Don't be embarrassed or too timid to request that restaurants adjust preparation of your food to fit your health and dietary needs.

Mock Spaghetti

1 cup cooked spaghetti squash (see recipe in this book for preparation instructions)
½ cup low fat 2% cottage cheese
1 cup light spaghetti sauce or spaghetti sauce recipe In this book
½ can mushrooms pieces and stems
1 small zuchinni (peeled if desired and chunked)

Combine spaghetti sauce, mushrooms and zuchinni in a small saucepan and heat, stirring occasionally. Place warm spaghetti squash on plate and top with cottage cheese. Pour spaghetti sauce mixture over squash and cottage cheese.

Yield: 2 servings
Per Serving: Calories: 127; Fat: 1.6 g; Carb: 17.5 g; Dietary Fiber: 3.9 g; Sugar: 7.7 g; Protein 11.7 g

Lifestyle Tip: Keep socializing with family and friends a priority **over** food.

Summer Steak Salad

2 ½ pounds sirloin, chunked
1 green bell pepper, sliced and grilled
1 yellow bell pepper, sliced and grilled
1 red bell pepper, sliced and grilled
1 avocado, diced
1 ripe mango, diced
2 tomatoes, chopped

Grill the sirloin and the peppers. Mix everything in a bowl and add your favorite dressing. Enjoy!

Yield: 4 servings
Per Serving: Calories: 343; Fat: 12.8 g; Carb: 11.4 g; Dietary Fiber: 3.5 g; Sugar: 6.2 g; Protein: 44.6 g

2nd Three Weeks Option: Add one ear of corn per person, washed and grilled lightly. Slice off kernels and mix with other ingredients.

Per Serving: Calories: 405; Fat: 13.6 g; Carb: 25.3 g; Dietary Fiber: 5.4 g; Sugar: 8.5 g; Protein: 46.9 g

Broiled Lemon Orange Roughy

3 tablespoons lemon juice
1 tablespoon Dijon mustard
1 tablespoon butter, melted

¼ teaspoon fresh coarse ground black pepper
1 teaspoon minced garlic
4 orange roughy fillet (6 ounce)
Lemon wedge

Preheat broiler. In a small mixing bowl, stir the lemon juice, mustard, butter and pepper until well blended; divide mixture in half. Place the fish fillets on a rack of a broiler pan that has been coated with cooking spray. Brush fillets with half the lemon juice mixture. Broil 5 1/2 inches from heat (with electric oven door partially opened) for 5 minutes or until fish flakes easily. Drizzle with the remaining half of lemon juice mixture. If desired, sprinkle with additional pepper and some salt; serve with lemon wedges.

Yield: 4 servings
Per Serving: Calories: 175; Fat: 5.1 g; Carb: 1.7 g; Dietary Fiber: 0.3 g; Sugar: 0.4 g; Protein 32.7 g

Mulligan Stew

1 pound lean ground beef, browned
2 medium turnips, chopped
1 head cabbage, chopped or shredded
1 can tomato soup
1 can water
Salt & pepper to taste

Put all ingredients into a soup pot. Simmer until vegetables are tender.

Yield: 6 servings   Serving Size: 1 cup
Per Serving: Calories: 201; Fat: 5.4 g; Carb: 16.4 g; Dietary Fiber: 4.3 g; Sugar: 9.6 g; Protein 22.5 g

2nd Three Weeks Option: Add 1-2 carrots, chopped
Per Serving: Calories: 210; Fat: 5.4 g Carb: 18.4 g; Dietary Fiber: 4.8 g; Sugar: 10.6 g; Protein 22.7g

Activity Tip: If you aren't motivated, come up with some "necessary" activities that force increased physical activity into your daily life. An example would be to take over walking and playing with the dog.

Citrus Tilapia

(Shown with Sweet Peas & Sundried Tomatoes)

2 (6 ounce) tilapia fillets
2 slices lemon
2 slices lime
1 slice orange
Dash of sea salt
Dash of fresh ground pepper

Preheat oven to 350° F. Squeeze the juice of the fruit on the tilapia with the salt and pepper. Cover and refrigerate overnight. Place in a baking dish with fruit on top and bake for 20 minutes or until done.

Yield: 2 servings
Per Serving: Calories: 146; Fat: 1.5 g; Carb: 1.3 g; Dietary Fiber: 0.3 g; Sugar: 0.5 g; Protein: 32.0 g

Asian Vegetarian Stir-Fry

Sauce:
2 tablespoons vegetable stock
1 tablespoon hoisin sauce
1 tablespoon soy sauce
2 teaspoons sesame oil
1 teaspoon honey
1 or 2 garlic cloves, finely minced
1 tablespoon freshly grated ginger

Stir-Fry:
Vegetable oil
1 medium sweet onion, thinly sliced
1 ½ cups sliced red bell peppers
1 ½ cups sliced green bell peppers
2 cups sugar snap peas
2 baby bok choy
1 ½ cups dried shiitake mushrooms, reconstituted and drained
Green onion, sliced for garnish

In a small dish, whisk together the sauce ingredients and set aside. In a large wok or skillet, add a small amount of vegetable oil and heat over medium-high heat. When a drop of water sizzles in the pan, add the onions and cook until lightly browned. Stir in the peppers and peas. Cut the baby bok choy in fourths lengthwise and then in 1 inch lengths. Add to wok and stir-fry until the bok choy begins to turn dark green, about 3 minutes. Add drained mushrooms and sauce. Cook just until warmed through. Also great with scallops, chicken, beef, pork, etc.

Yield: 6 servings   Serving Size: 1 cup
Per Serving: Calories: 161; Fat: 7.1 g; Carb: 22.3 g; Dietary Fiber: 5.7 g; Sugar: 10.6 g; Protein: 6.9 g

Chicken with Stir-Fry Vegetables

1 pound chicken cut in bite size pieces
1 bag frozen stir fry vegetables
1 packet stir fry seasoning mix (Sunbird Brand)
2 tablespoons soy sauce
0 calorie sweetener equal to 1 teaspoon sugar
⅓ cup water
2 tablespoons olive oil

In a small bowl, blend soy sauce, sweetener, water and seasoning mix. Place oil in a frying pan and saute chicken until pink is gone. Add vegetables and sauce mix. Continue to cook until vegetables are tender.

Yield: 6 servings   Serving Size: 1 cup
Per Serving: Calories: 193; Fat: 6.8 g; Carb: 7.9 g; Dietary Fiber: 2.1 g; Sugar: 2.1 g; Protein 23.5 g

Sloppy Joe

1 ½ pounds lean hamburger
1 cup sugar free bar-b-que sauce
1 cup tomato soup
0 calorie brown sugar sweetener of your choice equal to 1 tablespoon brown sugar

Brown hamburger. Add other ingredients and simmer.

Yield: 8 servings   Serving Size: ⅓ cup
Per Serving: Calories: 184; Fat: 6.6 g; Carb: 6.9 g; Dietary Fiber: 1.0 g; Sugar: 3.5 g; Protein 23.5 g

Citrus Shrimp

6 jumbo shrimp peeled, raw with tails on
1 tablespoon olive oil
1 tablespoon citrus seasoning

Heat oil over medium. Toss in shrimp and seasoning; heat until shrimp are done (turn pink).

Yield: 1 serving
Per Serving: Calories: 192; Fat: 10.2 g; Carb: 0.0 g; Dietary Fiber: 0.0 g; Sugar: 0.0 g; Protein: 23.7 g

Stuffed Peppers with Sausage

½ pound extra lean sausage
½ chopped onion
1 egg
¼ cup cheddar cheese
2 red peppers (sliced in half)
1 crushed garlic clove
½ teaspoon sea salt
⅛ teaspoon ground pepper

Preheat oven to 320° F. Brown sausage and onion in a skillet. Remove from heat and add the remaining ingredients, except the peppers. Place sausage mixture into pepper halves and bake for 15 minutes or until hot all the way through.

Yield: 2 servings   Serving Size: 2 halves
Per Serving: Calories: 296; Fat: 13.9 g; Carb: 14.3 g; Dietary Fiber: 1.2 g; Sugar: 3.8 g; Protein: 26.8 g

Healthy Tip: Avoid processed lunch meat, canned fruits and canned vegetables. Instead choose more raw, minimally cooked and frozen options as much as possible.

Indian Spiced Turkey Burgers

Topping:
¼ cup sour cream
¼ cup chopped cucumber

Burgers:
¼ cup finely chopped onion
1 medium fresh chopped jalapeno pepper
1 tablespoon chopped fresh mint or 1 teaspoon dried mint
½ teaspoon cumin
⅛ teaspoon garlic powder
¼ teaspoon salt
8 ounces lean ground turkey

Topping: Mix sour cream and cucumber in small bowl. Refrigerate until ready to serve. Burgers: Combine onion, pepper, mint, cumin, garlic and salt. Add ground turkey and mix well. Form mixture into two thick burgers about ¾ inch thick. Grill burgers. Top burgers with sour cream sauce and serve.

Yield: 2 servings   Serving Size: 1 burger with 2 tablespoons topping
Per Serving: Calories: 237; Fat: 14.3 g; Carb: 4.1 g; Dietary Fiber: 0.8 g; Sugar: 1.2 g; Protein: 23.7 g

Pizza – Chicken and Bacon

Crust:
2 cups shredded (and peeled – optional) zucchini
2 eggs
2 cups shredded mozzarella cheese
1 tablespoon Parmesan cheese

Preheat oven to 450° F. Shred a large zucchini. Squeeze out any excess water with a towel. Mix with all other ingredients except the Parmesan. Sprinkle a greased cookie sheet or baking stone with Parmesan cheese, like flouring a pan. Spread 2 cups shredded (and peeled - optional) zucchini mixture evenly, taking care not to let middle of crust get too thick. Bake for 12-15 minutes. Slice into 8 pieces.

Topping:
1 cup pizza sauce
2 (4 ounce) grilled chicken breasts – chunked
1 package Hormel cooked bacon
¼ cup chopped onion
1 talbespoon oregano
1 cup shredded mozzarella cheese

Preheat oven to 350° F. On baked zucchini crust, spread pizza sauce and add chicken, bacon and onion. Top with cheese and sprinkle with oregano. Bake for 15-20 minutes until toppings are done.

Yield: 8 servings   Serving Size: 1 slice
Per Serving: Calories: 271; Fat: 14.8 g; Carb: 6.9 g; Dietary Fiber: 1.1 g; Sugar: 2.0 g; Protein: 26.1 g

Stir Fry Beef and Vegetables

1 pound lean beef
1 tablespoon butter
¼ chopped onion
1 large zucchini
1 large summer (yellow) squash
2 teaspoons Safe Spice
2 tablespoons soy sauce

Melt butter in non-stick skillet. Sauté onion for about 10 minutes. Add squashes and meat. Sprinkle Safe Spice and soy sauce over meat and squash and stir. Serve over mock rice.

Yield: 4 servings   Serving Size: approximately ¾ cup
Per Serving: Calories: 269; Fat: 10.2 g; Carb: 6.6 g; Dietary Fiber: 2.3 g; Sugar: 1.8 g; Protein: 36.6 g

Cold Taco Pizza

Crust:

2 cups golden flax seed meal

1 tablespoon baking powder

1 teaspoon salt

0 calorie sweetener equal to 1 ½ tablespoons sugar

5 beaten eggs

½ cup water

⅓ cup olive oil

Preheat oven to 350° F. Whisk dry ingredients. Combine wet and dry ingredients, mixing well. Make sure there aren't stings of egg white hanging out in the batter. Let batter stand 2 – 3 (no more) minutes to thicken. Pour batter onto a pizza pan that is lined with oiled parchment paper. Start in the center and spread outward toward the edges of the pan. Bake for approximately 20 minutes until bread springs back when you touch the top and/or is visibly browned.

Topping:

1 pound ground beef

1 package taco seasoning mix

½ cup sour cream

½ cup picante or salsa

1 cup cheese (any combination of cheddar, mozzarella, Colby Jack)

¼ cup chopped onion

¼ cup sliced black olives

1 large chopped tomato

1 cup shredded lettuce

Brown ground beef and drain grease. Add taco seasoning mix and water per instructions on the package. Spread sour cream on top of baked pizza crust.   Add onion, olives, tomato and lettuce and top with salsa. Cut into 8 slices and serve.

Yield: 8 servings   Serving Size: 1 slice
Per Serving: Calories: 462; Fat: 32.7 g; Carb: 15.2 g; Dietary Fiber: 8.8 g; Sugar: 1.7 g; Protein: 31.6 g

2nd Three Weeks Option: Garnish each slice with 1 tablespoon light sour cream and 1 tablespoon guacamole.

Yield: 1 serving   Serving Size: 1 Slice
Per Serving: Calories: 503; Fat: 36.0 g; Carb: 16.7 g; Dietary Fiber: 9.4 g; Sugar: 2.4 g; Protein: 32.3 g

---

⚠ The caution sign identifies recipes that include caution items as ingredients. Some high fat caution items are milk, cheese, and nuts. Some high sugar (even though natural sugar) are pineapple and banana. Some high starchy vegetables are black beans and other legumes. These items are caution items for the 1st 3 weeks of maintenance. **Use these recipes in moderation and watch your morning weight closely, particularly during the 1st 3 weeks.**

Spicy Fried Chicken

4 (4 ounce) chicken breasts
2 eggs
2 cups crushed hot-n-spicy pork rinds
Salt and pepper to taste
2 tablespoons olive oil

Place olive oil in a pan and begin to heat. In a bowl, beat eggs and set aside. Dip chicken in eggs, and then roll in pork rinds until covered. Place chicken in frying pan and cook for about 15 minutes or until done. Salt and pepper to taste.

Yield: 4 servings   **Serving Size: 1 piece**
Per Serving: Calories: 353; Fat: 17.3 g; Carb: 0.2 g; Dietary Fiber: 0.2 g; Sugar: 0.0 g; Protein: 46.5 g

Chicken and Asparagus with Hollandaise Sauce

CAUTION: High FAT

1 cup mayonnaise
⅛ cup mustard
2 tablespoons A1 sauce
1 tablespoon Durkee Grill Creations Kansas City Steak
    Seasoning
6 (4 ounce) chicken breasts
1 bunch asparagus

Combine first four ingredients to make Hollandaise Sauce. Set aside ¾ cup of sauce for asparagus. Marinate chicken in remaining sauce for 2 hours, and then grill. Steam asparagus and drizzle with reserved Hollandaise Sauce.

Yield: 6 servings   **Serving Size: 1 piece with ⅙ of the asparagus**
Per Serving: Calories: 414; Fat: 14.4 g; Carb: 19.1 g; Dietary Fiber: 2.6 g; Sugar: 4.7 g; Protein: 36.1 g

> ⚠ The caution sign identifies recipes that include caution items as ingredients. Some high fat caution items are milk, cheese, and nuts. Some high sugar (even though natural sugar) are pineapple and banana. Some high starchy vegetables are black beans and other legumes. These items are caution items for the 1st 3 weeks of maintenance. **Use these recipes in moderation and watch your morning weight closely, particularly during the 1st 3 weeks.**

Pizza – Mexican

There are several pizza crusts/bread recipes in this book that may be used for pizza Crust. The nutritional value for this recipe is based on the Pizza Crust – Zucchini Based recipe. If you choose to use one of the other crusts, the nutritional value would be different, but should not be a problem since all of the recipes in this book are protocol compliant.

Crust:
2 cups shredded (and peeled – optional) zucchini
2 eggs
2 cups shredded mozzarella cheese
1 tablespoon Parmesan cheese

Preheat oven to 450° F. Shred a large zucchini. Squeeze out any excess water with a towel. Mix with all other ingredients except the Parmesan. Sprinkle a greased pizza pan or baking stone with Parmesan cheese, like flouring a pan. Spread 2 cups shredded (and peeled - optional) zucchini mixture evenly, taking care not to let middle of crust get too thick. Bake for 12-15 minutes.

Topping:
1 pound lean ground beef (drained)
1 package taco seasoning mix
½ cup fresh cut tomatoes
½ cup salsa
¼ cup chopped onion
¼ cup red peppers
1 cup shredded Monterey Jack cheese with jalapenos

Preheat oven to 350° F. Brown hamburger and add taco seasoning mix and the amount of water called for on the mix packet. In a blender, mix tomatoes and salsa. Spread the tomato puree on pizza crust for sauce. Top with taco meat, onion, peppers and cheese. Bake for about 15 minutes until toppings are done. Slice into 8 pieces and serve.

Yield: 8 servings   Serving Size: 1 slice
Per Serving: Calories: 291; Fat: 15.5 g; Carb: 6.5 g; Dietary Fiber: 0.8 g; Sugar: 1.8 g; Protein: 30.8 g

> ⚠ The caution sign identifies recipes that include caution items as ingredients. Some high fat caution items are milk, cheese, and nuts. Some high sugar (even though natural sugar) are pineapple and banana. Some high starchy vegetables are black beans and other legumes. These items are caution items for the 1st 3 weeks of maintenance. **Use these recipes in moderation and watch your morning weight closely, particularly during the 1st 3 weeks.**

Pork with Sugar Snap Peas

1 pound pork tenderloin, cut into ¼ inch thick slices
2 minced garlic cloves
2 teaspoons olive oil
10 ounces fresh or frozen sugar snap peas
6 tablespoons reduced-sodium soy sauce
4 tablespoons white wine vinegar
2 tablespoons sugar free maple syrup
1 ½ teaspoons ground ginger
½ teaspoon crushed red pepper flakes
1 red pepper (Optional)
1 cup broccoli (Optional)
1 cup bok choy (Optional)
½ cup mushrooms (Optional)

In a non-stick skillet, stir-fry pork and garlic in hot oil for 6 minutes or until meat is no longer pink. Remove pork from skillet. In same pan, cook the vegetables in soy sauce, vinegar, syrup, ginger and red pepper flakes for 4 minutes or until vegetables are crisp-tender. Return pork to pan; cook for 3 minutes or until glazed.

Without optional ingredients:
Yield: 4 servings   Serving Size: approximately 1 cup
Per Serving: Calories: 238; Fat: 6.5 g; Carb: 9.8 g; Dietary Fiber: 2.2 g; Sugar: 3.4 g; Protein: 33.3 g

With optional ingredients:
Yield: 4 servings   Serving Size: approximately 1 ½ cup
Per Serving: Calories: 251; Fat: 6.6 g; Carb: 12.2g; Dietary Fiber: 3.1 g; Sugar: 5.0 g; Protein: 34.1 g

Stuffed Peppers with Tuna
(Shown with European Tomatoes)

1 can tuna packed in water, drained
1 teaspoon Tony Chachere's Creole Seasoning
⅛ cup real mayonnaise
1 tablespoon Heinz Dill Relish
1 bell pepper
¼ cup shredded cheddar cheese

Preheat oven to 350° F. Cut pepper in half and remove pepper top and seeds. Mix tuna, seasoning, mayo and relish. Fill pepper halves and bake for 20 minutes. Sprinkle with cheese and bake a couple minutes longer until cheese is melted.

Yield: 2 servings   Serving Size: ½ pepper
Per Serving: Calories: 220; Fat: 10.3 g; Carb: 6.4 g; Dietary Fiber: 0.1 g; Sugar: 3.2 g; Protein: 24.7 g

Chicken Fettuccini

3 (4 ounce) chicken breasts
1 jar (15 ounce) Newman All Natural Alfredo Sauce
3 strips bacon, cooked and crumbled
1 (6 or 7 ounce) package Shirataki (fiber) Noodles*

*For best results when using Shirataki Noodles: Prior to use in a recipe, drain and thoroughly rinse the noodles with cold water. Place drained noodles in a non-stick frying pan and cook over medium heat, stirring occasionally, for approximately 10 minutes.

Grill or boil chicken, and cut into chunks. Warm Alf redo sauce in skillet and add crumbled bacon and prepared noodles. Cook down until most of the juice is gone. Add chicken and serve.

Yield: 3 servings   Serving Size: approximately 1 ½ cup
Per Serving: Calories: 368; Fat: 15.6 g; Carb: 1.6 g; Dietary Fiber: 0.0 g; Sugar: 0.2 g; Protein: 51.2 g

Nutrition Tip: Protein can help you lose weight by keeping you feeling full.

Show some caution with fatty meats, cheeses and whole dairy products.

Chicken Parmesan

(Shown with Wilted Spinach)

3 cups cooked spaghetti squash (see recipe in this book)
4 (4 ounce) grilled chicken breasts with Italian
    seasoning
2 cups light spaghetti sauce (or recipe in this book)
1 cup shredded Parmesan cheese
2 cloves garlic
2 tablespoons oregano

Add minced garlic and 1 tablespoon oregano to spaghetti sauce and let simmer. Cook spaghetti squash and drain well. Place ¾ cup spaghetti squash on dish, add ½ cup sauce, and sprinkle 3 tablespoons of cheese on top of the sauce. Place chicken breast on top of sauce and sprinkle 1 tablespoon Parmesan on top of chicken. Sprinkle with oregano; serve warm.

Yield: 4 servings   Serving Size: 1 piece
Per Serving: Calories: 367; Fat: 16.2 g; Carb: 10.4 g; Dietary Fiber: 1.0 g; Sugar: 0.3 g; Protein: 43.3 g

Chicken Fried "Rice"

2 (4 ounce) chicken breasts, cubed
1 tablespoon olive oil
½ green pepper
3 green onions
1 egg
3 cups shredded cauliflower
2 teaspoons soy sauce
1 package fried rice seasoning mix (Sun-Bird Brand)

In large skillet on medium heat, heat oil and cook chicken until done. Add onion, eggs, green pepper, cauliflower, soy sauce and seasoning. Cook about 5 minutes until cauliflower is almost done. Make a spot in the middle of pan, fry egg and scramble. Mix and serve.

Yield: 2 servings   Serving Size: approximately 1 ½ cups
Per Serving: Calories: 362; Fat: 13.2 g; Carb: 18.5 g; Dietary Fiber: 4.9 g; Sugar: 5.1 g; Protein: 42.8 g

Diet Tip: Include amino acids such as fish oil or flax seed oil daily.

Mexican Turkey Breast and Sweet Peppers

1 (2 pound) turkey breast
1 container (1 quart) fresh sweet peppers
½ onion, quartered
1 cup chicken or turkey broth
1 crushed garlic clove
1 packet taco seasoning mix

Preheat oven to 350° F.   In a roasting pan, place turkey breast. Rub top with ½ taco seasoning packet. Place peppers and onion around turkey breast. Mix broth, remaining seasoning and garlic clove and pour over vegetables. Bake for about 2 hours or until turkey breast is fully cooked.

Yield: 8 servings   Serving Size: 6 ounces turkey and ½ cup vegetables
Per Serving: Calories: 271; Fat: 4.3 g; Carb: 15.8 g; Dietary Fiber: 2.4 g; Sugar: 9.6 g; Protein: 40.2 g

Turkey Loaf

2 large eggs
2 tablespoons brown mustard
½ cup basic tomato sauce (see recipe in this book)
1 teaspoon dried oregano
1 teaspoon dried thyme
½ teaspoon sea salt
¼ teaspoon pepper
2 pounds ground turkey

Preheat oven to 400° F. Spray 9 x 13 baking dish with non-stick cooking spray. Lightly beat eggs. Add mustard, tomato sauce, oregano, thyme, salt and pepper. Mix well. Combine turkey but don't over mix or the loaf will be dry. Transfer mixture to baking dish and form into a loaf. Bake about 45 minutes. Let stand 5 minutes, divide into 8 pieces and serve.

Yield: 8 servings   **Serving Size: 1 piece**
Per Serving: Calories: 215; Fat: 6.9 g; Carb: 1.2 g; Dietary Fiber: 0.4 g; Sugar: 0.8 g; Protein: 35.1 g

Honey-Grilled Tenderloins

2 (¾ pound) pork tenderloins
⅓ cup low sodium soy sauce
5 cloves garlic, halved
4 tablespoons sugar free maple syrup
½ teaspoon ground ginger
0 calorie sweetener of choice equal to 2 tablespoons sugar
2 teaspoons dark sesame oil
Vegetable cooking spray

Trim fat from tenderloins. Place in a shallow container or large heavy zip lock plastic bag. Combine soy sauce, ginger and garlic; pour over the tenderloins. Cover and seal, then refrigerate at least 8 hours or overnight. Turn occasionally. Remove tenderloins from marinade, discarding the marinade.

Sauce:
Combine sweetener, sugar free maple syrup, and oil in a small saucepan; cooking on low heat, stirring constantly, until sweetener dissolves.

Place tenderloins on grill. Half way thru cooking, start brushing with sauce. Cook turning once and basting frequently with sauce mixture. Note: Basting mixture become thick when cool. Keep warm while grilling tenderloins by placing saucepan directly on the grill rack (or leave on stove).

Yield: 6 servings   **Serving Size: 4 ounces**
Per Serving: Calories: 191; Fat: 5.5 g; Carb: 3.8 g; Dietary Fiber: 0.2 g; Sugar: 0.3 g; Protein: 30.6 g

Miracle Cheese Penne

1 (6 or 7 ounce) package Shirataki (fiber) Noodles*
1 ½ cups small curd low fat 2 % cottage cheese
1 cup part-skim ricotta cheese
1 ¼ cups shredded part-skim mozzarella cheese,
    divided
3 tablespoons chopped parsley
2 teaspoons olive oil
1 medium Vidalia onion, chopped
4 cloves garlic, finely chopped
1 (15 ounce) can crushed tomatoes
1 (8 ounce) can tomato sauce
3 teaspoons Italian seasoning
¾ teaspoon sea salt
¼ teaspoon pepper
¼ cup grated Parmesan cheese

*For best results when using Shirataki Noodles: Prior to use in a recipe, drain and thoroughly rinse the noodles with cold water. Place drained noodles in a non-stick frying pan and cook over medium heat, stirring occasionally, for approximately 10 minutes.

Preheat oven to 400 ° F. Combine the cottage cheese, ricotta cheese, ½ cup mozzarella and parsley in a bowl and stir with a fork to incorporate and set aside. Heat the oil in the same pot over medium heat. Add the onion and cook, stirring occasionally, until translucent, about 5 minutes. Add the garlic and cook for 30 seconds more. Add the tomatoes, tomato sauce, Italian seasoning, salt and pepper. Bring to a boil, then reduce heat and simmer for 10 minutes until sauce thickens slightly. Return pasta to pot with sauce and turn off heat. Add cottage cheese mixture. Spray pan with non-stick spray. Place all ingredients in the 9 x 13. Top with remaining ¾ cup mozzarella and the Parmesan. Bake until heated through and cheese is melted, approximately 30 minutes. Let cool 5 minutes, cut into 12 pieces and serve.

Yield: 12 servings   Serving Size: 1 piece
Per Serving: Calories: 134; Fat: 6.3 g; Carb: 8.2 g; Dietary Fiber: 1.6 g; Sugar: 3.5 g; Protein: 11.4 g

Lifestyle Tip: Don't have anxiety over time. We all have all the time there is and we can't get any more, so relax as there is no need to pressure ourselves any more than the world already does.

Fried Chicken

½ cup almond meal
½ cup Parmesan cheese
1 egg
3 (4 ounce) chicken breasts

Mix almond meal and Parmesan cheese. Dip chicken breast into egg and roll in the mixture. Bake or fry in olive oil.

Yield: 3 servings   Serving Size: 4 ounces
Per Serving: Calories: 399; Fat: 22.5 g; Carb: 4.2 g; Dietary Fiber: 1.9 g; Sugar: 0.9 g; Protein: 44.4 g

Cashew Chicken

16 ounces boneless chicken breasts, skinned
4 tablespoons olive oil, divided

Marinade:
1 egg white
1 teaspoon salt
2 ounces cashew nuts
2 tablespoons olive oil
1 teaspoon cashew flour

Cut chicken into ½ inch cubes. Add the marinade ingredients to the chicken cubes, mixing together and adding cashew flour last. Allow the chicken to marinate in the refrigerator for 15 – 20 minutes. Heat the wok (or large frying pan) and add 3 tablespoons of oil. When the oil is ready, add the chicken cubes and stir-fry on medium heat, stirring quickly to ensure that the chicken does not stick to the wok, until it turns white. Remove the chicken from the wok and set aside. Clean the wok with a paper towel and add one tablespoon of oil. When the oil is ready, add the cashews and stir-fry them for about one minute. Add the chicken and stir together. Remove from wok and serve.

Yield: 4 servings   Serving Size: 4 ounces
Per Serving: Calories: 480; Fat: 35.2 g; Carb: 4.7 g; Dietary Fiber: 0.4 g; Sugar: 0.8 g; Protein: 35.9 g

---

The caution sign identifies recipes that include caution items as ingredients. Some high fat caution items are milk, cheese, and nuts. Some high sugar (even though natural sugar) are pineapple and banana. Some high starchy vegetables are black beans and other legumes. These items are caution items for the 1st 3 weeks of maintenance. **Use these recipes in moderation and watch your morning weight closely, particularly during the 1st 3 weeks.**

Parmesan Crusted Tilapia

4 (5 ounce) tilapia fillets
1 cup shredded Parmesan cheese
2 tablespoons mayonnaise
1 teaspoon oregano
1 teaspoon fresh pressed garlic
1 teaspoon paprika
1 teaspoon onion powder

Preheat oven to 350° F. Place tilapia on baking sheet. Combine other ingredients and spread on top of fillets. Bake for 30 minutes or until done. To grill, roll tilapia in mixture to coat all sides. Grill and serve.

Yield: 4 servings   Serving Size: 1 fillet
Per Serving: Calories: 260; Fat: 11.0 g; Carb: 4.0 g; Dietary Fiber: 0.4 g; Sugar: 1.0 g; Protein: 36.5 g

> *Diet Tip:* Eat REAL food: real fruits, real fats (olive oil, almonds, regular salad dressing, real cream) and real meat (seafood, pork, chicken, hot wings, fish) instead of highly processed foods.

Shrimp Scampi and Pasta

1 (6 or 7 ounce) package Shirataki (fiber) Noodles*
2 tablespoons butter
1 clove garlic, crushed
1 tablespoon lemon juice, fresh squeezed if possible
2 teaspoons dried parsley
¾ pound shrimp, drained and peeled

*For best results when using Shirataki Noodles: Prior to use in a recipe, drain and thoroughly rinse the noodles with cold water. Place drained noodles in a non-stick frying pan and cook over medium heat, stirring occasionally, for approximately 10 minutes.

Place noodles in a large skillet with all ingredients but the shrimp. Toss noodles for about 2 minutes. Clear a spot in the center of the pan and add shrimp. Place a cover on the pan and cook about 5 minutes until shrimp is done. Turn burner on low until you are ready to serve.

Yield: 2 servings   Serving Size: ½ of mixture
Per Serving: Calories: 283; Fat: 13.4 g; Carb: 3.0 g; Dietary Fiber: 0.1 g; Sugar: 0.2 g; Protein: 35.9 g

Sundried Tomato Glazed Salmon
(Shown with Almond Broccoli & Rice)

1 pound salmon
1 cup Sundried Tomato Vinaigrette dressing

Place salmon in a container and pour the dressing over it. Marinate for a minimum of 2 hours. Grill or bake the salmon. Discard remaining dressing/marinade. For baking, preheat oven to 350° F for about 30 minutes. Salmon is done when you stick with a fork and the meat flakes. Great served with Mock Rice and Almond Broccoli (both recipes in this book).

Yield: 4 servings   Serving Size: 4 ounces
Per Serving: Calories: 299; Fat: 19.5 g; Carb: 3.0 g; Dietary Fiber: 0.0 g; Sugar: 3.0 g; Protein: 25.1 g

Diet Tip: Include live food, for example, uncooked, fruit or vegetables, and natural organic protein, (preferably not injected with hormones or antibiotics) at every meal.

Meatless Spaghetti

1 (6 or 7 ounce) package Shirataki (fiber) Noodles*
½ cup low fat 2% cottage cheese
1 cup tomato sauce
1 tablespoon Italian seasoning
1 teaspoon garlic, minced
¾ teaspoon sea salt
2 tablespoons Parmesan cheese

*For best results when using Shirataki Noodles: Prior to use in a recipe, drain and thoroughly rinse the noodles with cold water. Place drained noodles in a non-stick frying pan and cook over medium heat, stirring occasionally, for approximately 10 minutes.

Place tomato sauce, Italian seasoning, garlic and salt in skillet and simmer. Heat noodles. Place cottage cheese over hot noodles and top with spaghetti sauce. Sprinkle on Parmesan cheese.

Yield: 2 servings   Serving Size: approximately 1 ½ cups
Per Serving: Calories: 114; Fat: 2.9 g; Carb: 11.4 g; Dietary Fiber: 2.3 g; Sugar: 5.1 g; Protein: 11.4 g

Spaghetti with Meatballs

1 pound lean ground beef
1 egg
¼ cup Parmesan cheese
1 teaspoon oregano
1 teaspoon garlic powder
1 tablespoon onion powder
1½ teaspoons salt
½ teaspoon pepper
1 (6 or 7 ounce) package Shirataki (fiber) Noodles*
½ cup low fat 2% cottage cheese
1 cup tomato sauce
1 zucchini chunked
Parmesan cheese

*For best results when using Shirataki Noodles: Prior to use in a recipe, drain and thoroughly rinse the noodles with cold water. Place drained noodles in a non-stick frying pan and cook over medium heat, stirring occasionally, for approximately 10 minutes.

Combine ground beef, egg, Parmesan cheese, oregano, garlic powder, onion powder salt and pepper and mix well. Roll into 8 meat balls and fry in pan until all sides are browned. Place tomato sauce and zucchini in skillet and simmer until zucchini is tender. Heat noodles, add cottage cheese. Place noodles on serving dish and top with tomato sauce. Add the meatballs and sprinkle on Parmesan cheese.

Yield: 8 servings   Serving Size: approximately 1 cup pasta with 2 meatballs
Per Serving: Calories: 316; Fat: 10.7 g; Carb: 9.5 g; Dietary Fiber: 1.9 g; Sugar: 4.5 g; Protein: 43.9 g

Mexican Tilapia

4 (4 ounce) tilapia fillets
2 tablespoons mayonnaise
½ cup salsa

Mix salsa and mayonnaise. Marinate fish for a minimum of 2 hours. Place on grill and cook 15 – 20 minutes until done.

Yield: 4 servings   Serving Size: 1 fillet
Per Serving: Calories: 132; Fat: 3.5 g; Carb: 3.8 g; Dietary Fiber: 0.5 g; Sugar: 1.5 g; Protein: 21.8 g

Chicken Paprikash

2 (4 ounce) chicken breasts, cooked and cubed
⅔ cup water
¾ teaspoon minced garlic
½ yellow bell pepper, chopped
½ red bell pepper, chopped
¼ cup onion, chopped
1 medium tomato, coarsely chopped
1 tablespoon paprika
1 teaspoon sea salt
⅛ teaspoon cayenne pepper
½ cup sour cream
1 (6 or 7 ounce) package Shirataki (fiber) Noodles*

*For best results when using Shirataki Noodles: Prior to use in a recipe, drain and thoroughly rinse the noodles with cold water. Place drained noodles in a non-stick frying pan and cook over medium heat, stirring occasionally, for approximately 10 minutes.

Cook chicken breasts in ½ cup water. When done, remove chicken to cool and reserve broth. Cube chicken. Sautee garlic, peppers, onion and tomato in ¼ cup of the chicken broth. Add chicken, paprika, salt, pepper and miracle noodles. Simmer for 20 minutes. Stir in sour cream right before serving.

Yield: 4 servings   Serving Size: approximately ¾ cup
Per Serving: Calories: 193; Fat: 10.6 g; Carb: 6.2 g; Dietary Fiber: 1.6 g; Sugar: 2.0 g; Protein: 18.1 g

Garlic and Herb Shrimp Kabobs

1 pound raw shrimp – shelled with tails on
2 bell peppers (red, yellow, orange or green)
1 pint whole mushrooms
1 pint grape tomatoes
⅛ cup olive oil
1 packet Good Seasons Herb and Garlic dressing mix

In a large container combine all the above ingredients. Place in the refrigerator for two hours. Place on 4 skewers and grill until shrimp are done or place in a non-stick skillet and sauté until done.

Yield: 4 servings   Serving Size: 1 skewer
Per Serving: Calories: 237; Fat: 10.6 g; Carb: 9.3 g;
Dietary Fiber: 2.3 g; Sugar: 3.8 g; Protein: 26.2 g

Healthy Tuna Salad

1 can water packed tuna, drained
1 apple, chopped
2 tablespoons mayonnaise
1 stalk celery or to taste
Salt and pepper to taste

Combine tuna, apple, mayo, celery, salt and pepper. Serve with celery or romaine lettuce leafs.

Yield: 2 servings   Serving Size: approximately ½ cup
Per Serving: Calories: 190; Fat: 5.7 g; Carb: 13.3 g; Dietary Fiber: 1.8 g; Sugar: 8.3 g; Protein: 21.4 g

Turkey Salad

3 hard-boiled eggs, chopped
3 cups cooked turkey meat
½ cup sweet relish
⅔ cup Dijon mayonnaise
½ cup mayonnaise
2 stalks celery, finely chopped
2 tablespoons sweet onion, finely chopped
Sea salt and pepper to taste

In a large bowl, thoroughly mix the eggs, turkey, pickle relish, prepared sandwich and salad sauce and mayonnaise. Chill in the refrigerator approximately 3 hours before serving.
Optional additions: apples, pecans, almonds, walnut, grapes

Yield: 8 servings   Serving Size: ½ cup
Per Serving: Calories: 310; Fat: 22.6 g; Carb: 10.4 g; Dietary Fiber: 0.3 g; Sugar: 5.4 g; Protein: 17.7 g

> ⚠ The caution sign identifies recipes that include caution items as ingredients. Some high fat caution items are milk, cheese, and nuts. Some high sugar (even though natural sugar) are pineapple and banana. Some high starchy vegetables are black beans and other legumes. These items are caution items for the 1st 3 weeks of maintenance. **Use these recipes in moderation and watch your morning weight closely, particularly during the 1st 3 weeks.**

Salads

Buffalo Chicken Salad

1 cup mixed salad greens
⅛ cup mozzarella cheese (shredded)
⅛ cup shredded cheddar cheese
1 (4 ounce) chicken breast, baked (keep warm)
2 tablespoons Ranch dressing
1 tablespoon Frank's Buffalo Wing Sauce or to taste

Toss the above together and serve.

Yield: 1 serving
Per Serving: Calories: 329; Fat: 12.0 g; Carb: 8.8 g; Dietary Fiber: 0.2 g; Sugar: 2.3 g; Protein: 44.6 g

Strawberry-Bacon Spinach Salad

1 pound fresh baby spinach
2 cups fresh strawberries, quartered
8 bacon strips, cooked and crumbled
¼ cup red onion, chopped
¼ cup chopped walnuts OR toasted almonds
    (350 ° F for 8-10 minutes to toast almonds)
0 calorie sweetener of your choice equal to ½ cup sugar
1 cup mayonnaise
¼ cup raspberry vinegar

Combine spinach, strawberries, bacon, onion and walnuts in salad bowl. In a small bowl, beat or cream mayonnaise, sweetener and vinegar. Toss dressing with salad just before serving.

Yield: 6 servings   Serving Size: 1 cup
Per Serving: Calories: 273; Fat: 20.6 g; Carb: 19.0 g; Dietary Fiber: 3.1 g; Sugar: 5.5 g; Protein: 7.7 g

Make Ahead Salad

1 head Romaine lettuce, chopped
½ head iceberg lettuce, chopped
2 stalks broccoli, chopped
½ head cauliflower, chopped
1 bunch green onions, chopped
1 cup light mayonnaise
8 ounces sharp cheddar cheese, grated
12 ounces bacon, cooked and crumbled
0 calorie sweetener equal to 2 tablespoons sugar
1 package dry Hidden Valley Buttermilk Ranch Dressing mix

Layer vegetables in large salad bowl. Mix mayonnaise, sweetener and dry dressing mix and pour on top of vegetables. Cover and chill up to 24 hours. Just before serving, toss bacon and cheese over salad and mix together.

Yield: 12 servings   Serving Size: approximately ¾ cup
Per Serving: Calories: 221; Fat: 16.8 g; Carb: 7.8 g; Dietary Fiber: 1.8 g; Sugar: 1.5 g; Protein: 10.4 g

Fruit & Chicken Viniagerette

2 cups mixed lettuce greens
½ apple sliced into bite sized pieces
⅛ cup grapes
1 tablespoon dried cranberries
1 (4 ounce) grilled chicken breast, sliced
1 tablespoon Sweet Roasted Walnuts (see recipe in this book), chopped
2 tablespoons Kraft Raspberry Vinaigrette Dressing

Top lettuce with apple, grapes, cranberries, chicken and chopped nuts. Toss with dressing and enjoy.

Yield: 1 serving
Per Serving: Calories: 357; Fat: 12.0 g; Carb: 24.3 g; Dietary Fiber: 3.9 g; Sugar: 19.5 g; Protein: 38.3 g

---

⚠ The caution sign identifies recipes that include caution items as ingredients. Some high fat caution items are milk, cheese, and nuts. Some high sugar (even though natural sugar) are pineapple and banana. Some high starchy vegetables are black beans and other legumes. These items are caution items for the 1st 3 weeks of maintenance. **Use these recipes in moderation and watch your morning weight closely, particularly during the 1st 3 weeks.**

Berry Spinach Salad

¾ cup almonds, blanched and slivered
1 pound baby spinach, rinsed
¼ cup dried cranberries
½ cup fresh blueberries
1 tablespoon poppy seeds
0 calorie sweetener of choice equal to ⅓ cup sugar
2 teaspoons minced onion
¼ teaspoon paprika
¼ cup white wine vinegar
¼ cup cider vinegar
½ cup olive oil
Salt to taste
Optional: Add 4 ounces of grilled chicken to individual servings to make this into a meal.

Preheat oven to 350° F. Toast the almonds for about 10 minutes until lightly browned. Remove from heat and let cool. In a large bowl, combine the spinach with the toasted almonds, cranberries and blueberries.   In a medium bowl, whisk together the poppy seeds, sweetener, onion, paprika, white wine vinegar, cider vinegar, and vegetable oil. Toss with spinach just before serving.

Without chicken:

Yield: 8 servings   Serving Size: approximately 1 cup

Per Serving: Calories: 213; Fat: 18.9 g; Carb: 9.2 g; Dietary Fiber: 4.1 g; Sugar: 2.1 g; Protein: 5.4 g

With chicken:

Per Serving: Calories: 384; Fat: 22.3 g; Carb: 9.2 g; Dietary Fiber: 4.1 g; Sugar: 2.1 g; Protein: 38.3 g

---

⚠ The caution sign identifies recipes that include caution items as ingredients. Some high fat caution items are milk, cheese, and nuts. Some high sugar (even though natural sugar) are pineapple and banana. Some high starchy vegetables are black beans and other legumes. These items are caution items for the 1st 3 weeks of maintenance. **Use these recipes in moderation and watch your morning weight closely, particularly during the 1st 3 weeks.**

Diet Tip: Take advantage of what is in season for optimum taste and nutritional value. Enjoy fresh fruits and fresh vegetables whenever possible: salads, soups, and yogurt.

Mozzarella and Tomato Salad

2 large ripe tomatoes (peeled and sliced ¼" thick)
8 ounces fresh mozzarella, sliced ¼" thick
¼ teaspoon salt
2 tablespoons extra virgin olive oil
8 fresh basil leaves
1 teaspoon balsamic vinegar

Arrange the tomato and mozzarella slices on a platter or on 8 individual salad plates, overlapping the slices and fanning them out to resemble a deck of playing cards. Drizzle with oil, salt and pepper to taste. Garnish with basil cut or torn into small bits. Serve immediately.

Yield: 8 servings   Serving Size: approximately ¼ tomato and 1 slice of cheese
Per Serving: Calories: 124; Fat: 9.2 g; Carb: 2.9 g; Dietary Fiber: 0.6 g; Sugar: 1.4 g; Protein: 7.8 g

Healthy Tip: Fiber helps keep you full longer.

Fruit Salad with Cottage Cheese and Creamy Peanut Butter Dressing

Dressing:
¼ cup drained blended pineapple (no sugar)
1 tablespoon creamy peanut butter
¼ cup whipped topping
2 tablespoons reduced fat sour cream
0 calorie sweetener of choice equal to 2 teaspoons sugar

Salad:
1 cup leaf lettuce of choice
1 cup small curd low fat 2% cottage cheese
½ cup strawberries, sliced
½ kiwi, sliced
2 ounces mandarin oranges, drained

Dressing: Mix pineapple, peanut butter, whipped topping and sour cream in a medium bowl until well combined. **Salad:** Arrange lettuce leaves on 2 salad plates. Top each plate with ½ cup cottage cheese. Garnish with fresh fruit and spoon creamy peanut butter dressing over all.

Yield: 2 servings   Serving Size: 1 plate
Per Serving: Calories: 261; Fat: 10.1 g; Carb: 25.7 g; Dietary Fiber: 3.7 g; Sugar: 14.9 g; Protein: 19.8 g

Mandarin Orange Lettuce Salad

Salad:
1 head of iceberg lettuce
1 head of Romaine lettuce
1 (10 ounce) package of spinach
½ red onion or to taste, sliced
1 small can mandarin oranges, drained
1 cup celery, chopped
2.5 ounces slivered almonds, toasted
1 (20 ounce) can pineapple chunks, drained

Poppy Seed Dressing:
0 calorie sweetener of choice equal to ¾ cup sugar
1 teaspoon dry mustard
1 teaspoon sea salt
⅓ cup red wine vinegar
1 cup olive oil
1½ tablespoons poppy seeds

In a blender*, combine sweetener, dry mustard, vinegar and salt. Slowly add oil and poppy seeds.

* Must use a blender, not a shaker jar, to keep the dressing from separating.

Mix together salad greens, red onion, pineapple chunks, mandarin oranges and toasted almonds in a salad bowl. Top with Poppy Seed Dressing and serve immediately.

Yield: 10 servings   Serving Size: approximately 1 cup
Per Serving: Calories: 305; Fat: 26.2 g; Carb: 17.4 g; Dietary Fiber: 4.6 g; Sugar: 10.1 g; Protein: 4.3 g

> The caution sign identifies recipes that include caution items as ingredients. Some high fat caution items are milk, cheese, and nuts. Some high sugar (even though natural sugar) are pineapple and banana. Some high starchy vegetables are black beans and other legumes. These items are caution items for the 1st 3 weeks of maintenance. **Use these recipes in moderation and watch your morning weight closely, particularly during the 1st 3 weeks.**

Lifestyle Tip: Get a good night's sleep! Approximately eight hours is recommended and has been associated with maintaining a healthy weight.

Traditional Taco Salad

1 pound lean ground beef
½ cup cheddar cheese
½ cup salsa
½ cup sour cream
1 package taco seasoning (1 cup water with seasoning)
1 small tomato, chopped
9 cups lettuce

Cook lean ground beef, drain fat. Add taco seasoning, mix with water and let simmer. Either make individual plates (as pictured) or mix in a bowl. Add lettuce, cheese, tomatoes, and ground beef. Toss with salsa. Drop sour cream on top or serve on the side. Serve immediately.

Yield: 6 servings   Serving Size: approximately 1 ½ cups
Per Serving: Calories: 252; Fat: 12.3 g; Carb: 7.6 g; Dietary Fiber: 1.2 g; Sugar: 2.2 g; Protein: 27.3 g

....
Healthy Tip: Reduce your level of stress.
....

Caesar Salad

1 head Romaine lettuce, torn

Dressing:
3 cloves garlic, peeled
¾ cup low fat mayonnaise
5 anchovy fillets, minced
2 tablespoons grated Parmesan cheese divided
1 teaspoon Worcestershire sauce
1 teaspoon Dijon mustard
1 tablespoon lemon juice
Salt to taste
Ground black pepper to taste

Mince 3 cloves of garlic and combine in a small bowl with mayonnaise, anchovies, Parmesan cheese, and Worcestershire sauce, mustard and lemon juice. Season to taste with salt and black pepper. Place torn lettuce in a bowl and toss with the dressing.

Yield: 6 servings   Serving Size: approximately ¾ cup
Per Serving: Calories: 119; Fat: 10.8 g; Carb: 3.0 g; Dietary Fiber: 0.1 g; Sugar: 0.3 g; Protein: 1.8 g

Oriental Slaw Salad

CAUTION:
High FAT

2 pounds or 1 head cabbage, shredded
4 to 6 green onions with top, chopped
1 (2.5 ounce) package of sliced almonds, toasted
1 cup salted sunflower seeds, no shells
1 package of beef flavored Ramen noodles (use ONLY
the seasoning packet for the 1st three weeks)

Dressing:
⅓ cup white vinegar
½ cup oil
0 calorie sweetener equal to ½ cup sugar
Ramen Seasoning packet

Combine vinegar, oil, sweetener, and seasoning packet. Toss with other ingredients right before serving.

Yield: 10 servings   Serving Size: ½ cup
Per Serving: Calories: 198; Fat: 16.5 g; Carb: 10.9 g; Dietary Fiber: 3.7 g; Sugar: 4.2 g; Protein: 3.6 g

2nd Three Weeks Option: Crumble up the dry noodles from the Ramen package into the salad with the rest of the ingredients.

Yield: 10 serving   Serving Size: ½ cup
Per Serving: Calories: 225; Fat: 17.9 g; Carb: 14.5 g; Dietary Fiber: 3.9 g; Sugar: 3.6 g; Protein: 4.6 g

⚠ The caution sign identifies recipes that include caution items as ingredients. Some high fat caution items are milk, cheese, and nuts. Some high sugar (even though natural sugar) are pineapple and banana. Some high starchy vegetables are black beans and other legumes. These items are caution items for the 1st 3 weeks of maintenance. **Use these recipes in moderation and watch your morning weight closely, particularly during the 1st 3 weeks.**

Salad Dressings, Sauces & Toppings

Note: Since many salads and salad dressings have oils, mayonnaise, cheese, nuts, etc. in the recipes, it should not be a surprise that these recipes are more likely to be labeled High Fat. You should limit your daily intake of caution items overall and watch the scale closely. Moderation is the key to success in maintenance and beyond.

Salad Dressings

Poppy Seed Dressing
(Shown with Mandarin Orange Chicken Salad)

1 cup olive oil
0 calorie sweetener of choice equal to ¾ cup sugar
1 teaspoon dry mustard
1 teaspoon sea salt
⅓ cup red wine vinegar
1½ tablespoons poppy seeds

In a blender*, combine sweetener, dry mustard, vinegar and salt. Slowly add oil and poppy seeds.

* Must use a blender, not a shaker jar, to keep the dressing from separating.

Yield: 1 ⅓ cups, 10 servings   Serving Size: 2 tablespoons
Per Serving: Calories: 183; Fat: 20.3 g; Carb: 1.2 g; Dietary Fiber: 0.2 g; Sugar: 0.2 g; Protein: 0.3 g

⚠ The caution sign identifies recipes that include caution items as ingredients. Some high fat caution items are milk, cheese, and nuts. Some high sugar (even though natural sugar) are pineapple and banana. Some high starchy vegetables are black beans and other legumes. These items are caution items for the 1st 3 weeks of maintenance. **Use these recipes in moderation and watch your morning weight closely, particularly during the 1st 3 weeks.**

Sweet French Dressing

CAUTION: High FAT

⅔ cup tomato paste – no added sugar
1½ cups canola oil
⅓ cup water plus 3 tablespoons
⅔ cup and ¼ cup white vinegar
½ teaspoon dried onion powder
½ teaspoon dried garlic powder
½ tablespoon ground mustard powder
 0 calorie sweetener of choice equal to ⅓ cup to ½ cup sugar based on your preference
⅛ teaspoon sea salt

Place tomato paste in a large bowl. Slowly blend tomato paste with the canola oil. Add remaining ingredients and keep stored in an airtight container in the refrigerator.

Yield: 3 ½ cups, 56 servings   Serving Size: 2 tablespoons
Per Serving: Calories: 114; Fat: 12.1 g; Carb: 1.5 g; Dietary Fiber: 0.3 g; Sugar: 0.8 g; Protein: 0.3 g

> ⚠ The caution sign identifies recipes that include caution items as ingredients. Some high fat caution items are milk, cheese, and nuts. Some high sugar (even though natural sugar) are pineapple and banana. Some high starchy vegetables are black beans and other legumes. These items are caution items for the 1st 3 weeks of maintenance. **Use these recipes in moderation and watch your morning weight closely, particularly during the 1st 3 weeks.**

Creamy Peanut Butter Dressing
(Shown with Fruit Salad and Cottage Cheese)

1 cup drained blended pineapple (no sugar)
¼ cup creamy peanut butter
1 cup whipped topping
½ cup reduced fat sour cream
0 calorie sweetener equal to 1 tablespoon sugar

Mix pineapple, peanut butter, whipped topping and sour cream in a medium bowl until well combined.

Yield: 8 servings   Serving Size: ¼ cup
Per Serving: Calories: 97; Fat: 7.6 g; Carb: 5.9 g; Dietary Fiber: 0.8 g; Sugar: 3.3 g; Protein: 2.8 g

Caesar Salad Dressing

½ cup nonfat Greek yogurt
⅓ cup low fat 2% cottage cheese
¼ cup freshly grated Parmesan cheese
5 teaspoons white wine vinegar
½ teaspoon Worcestershire sauce
1 clove crushed garlic
⅛ teaspoon sea salt to taste
Ground pepper to taste

Mix all ingredients well.

Yield: 1 cup   Serving Size: 2 tablespoons
Per Serving: Calories: 33; Fat: 1.4 g; Carb: 1.3 g; Dietary Fiber: 0.0 g; Sugar: 0.7g; Protein: 3.7 g

Ranch Dressing

1 cup 2% milk
1 tablespoon white vinegar or lemon juice
1 cup low fat 2% cottage cheese
1 packet Hidden Valley Ranch Dressing mix

Pour vinegar or lemon juice in a measuring cup. Add skim milk until liquid is up to the one cup line.
Let stand for 5 minutes. Put into blender with dressing mix and cottage cheese. Blend until smooth.

Yield: 2 cups, 16 servings   Serving Size: 2 tablespoons
Per Serving: Calories: 26; Fat: 0.6 g; Carb: 2.2 g; Dietary Fiber: 0.0 g; Sugar: 0.8 g; Protein: 2.4 g

Western Dressing

0 calorie sweetener of your choice equal to ½ cup sugar
½ teaspoon sea salt
⅛ teaspoon paprika
¼ teaspoon chili powder
¼ teaspoon celery seed
¼ teaspoon dry mustard
¼ teaspoon onion powder
¼ cup vinegar
⅓ cup Heinz Reduced Sugar Ketchup or use one of the ketchup recipes in this book
½ cup olive oil

Combine in blender or food processor. Chill.

Yield: 1 ⅓ cups, 10 servings   Serving Size: 2 tablespoons
Per Serving: Calories: 51; Fat: 5.4 g; Carb: 1.7 g; Dietary Fiber: 0.0 g; Sugar: 1.0 g; Protein: 0.0 g

Sauces (Condiments and Other Basics)

Heinzy Ketchup

6 ounce can tomato paste
½ cup water
¼ cup white vinegar
0 calorie sweetener of choice equal to 5 teaspoons sugar
¼ teaspoon onion powder
1 teaspoon sea salt
Very tiny pinch or up to ⅛ teaspoon each, ground cloves, cinnamon and garlic powder

Mix all ingredients well.

Yield: 1 ½ cups, 24 servings   Serving Size: 1 tablespoon
Per Serving: Calories: 8; Fat: 0.0 g; Carb: 1.7 g; Dietary Fiber: 0.3 g; Sugar: 1.0 g; Protein: 0.4 g

Red Pepper Sauce:

8 ounces roasted red peppers (jarred are fine)
1 teaspoon tamari or Spike vegetable seasoning

Blend roasted red peppers in blender with tamari. Pour into saucepan and heat through. Great served over cabbage.

Yield: ¾ cup, 6 servings   Serving Size: 2 tablespoons
Per Serving: Calories: 10.0; Fat: 0.0 g; Carb: 2.4 g; Dietary Fiber: 0.5 g; Sugar: 1.7 g; Protein: 0.5 g

Spicy Cocktail Sauce

½ cup Low Sugar Heinz or sugar free ketchup
1 tablespoon horseradish
1 teaspoon hot sauce (optional)
¼ teaspoon lemon zest
½ teaspoon lemon juice

Mix all ingredients well. Keep in refrigerator for up to 5 days.

Yield: 4 servings   Serving Size: 2 tablespoons
Per Serving: Calories: 12; Fat: 0.1 g; Carb: 2.6 g; Dietary Fiber: 0.1 g; Sugar: 2.4 g; Protein: 0.1 g

Sugar Free Ketchup

6 ounces tomato paste
⅔ cup cider vinegar
⅓ cup water
 0 calorie sweetener of choice equal to ⅓ cup sugar
2 tablespoons onion powder
2 cloves garlic
1 teaspoon salt
⅛ teaspoon ground Spike seasoning
    (May use allspice to substitute for Spike)
⅛ teaspoon ground cloves
⅛ teaspoon pepper

Put all ingredients in blender and blend until the onion disappears. Scrape into a container with a tight lid and store in the refrigerator.

Yield: 2 cups   **Serving Size: 2 tablespoons**
Per Serving: Calories: 14; Fat: 0.1 g; Carb: 3.5 g; Dietary Fiber: 0.5 g; Sugar: 1.6 g; Protein: 0.6 g

Very Low Sugar Bar-B-Que Sauce

1 tablespoon olive oil
1 small Vidalia onion, minced
½ cup water
¼ teaspoon garlic powder
1 (6 ounce) small can tomato paste
1 (12 ounce) can diet root beer
¼ cup low sugar or sugar free catsup
3 tablespoons mustard
1 tablespoon Worcestershire sauce
1 pinch ground cloves
1 tablespoon plain cocoa
¼ teaspoon chili powder
¼ teaspoon cinnamon
¼ teaspoon sea salt
¼ teaspoon pepper
2 teaspoons Liquid Smoke
Hot sauce to taste (start with ½ teaspoon if you like some kick)

> **Diet Tip:** More sugar free products become available every day. Websites like Nature's Hollow are a good place to start.

Melt the butter in a 2 qt. pan. Add the onion and cook over medium heat until soft, about 3-5 minutes. Add the rest of the ingredients, plus about half of a cup of water. Stir well. Simmer for 20-30 minutes. It will cook down a bit and flavors will combine. Taste to check and adjust the seasonings to your preference.

Yield: 2 ½ cups, 10 servings   Serving Size: ¼ cup
Per Serving: Calories: 56.0; Fat: 2.5 g; Carb: 7.8 g; Dietary Fiber: 1.6 g; Sugar: 4.5 g; Protein: 2.0 g

Basic Italian Tomato Sauce

1 (14.5 ounce) can Hunts fire roasted tomatoes
3 tablespoons tomato paste
¼ cup roasted peppers
¼ teaspoon salt
¼ teaspoon oregano
½ teaspoon garlic powder

Combine ingredients and mix well. For a meat sauce, add 1 pound browned and drained lean ground beef.

Yield: 4 servings   Serving Size: ½ cup
Per Serving: Calories: 44; Fat: 0.1 g; Carb: 9.1 g; Dietary Fiber: 1.5 g; Sugar: 5.4 g; Protein: 1.5 g

Meat Spaghetti Sauce for a Crowd

1 pound lean ground beef
1 can (28 oz.) crushed tomatoes
1 can (15oz) tomato sauce
1 can (3 oz.) tomato paste
1 can (10 oz.) tomato soup
1 small chopped onion
1 teaspoon minced garlic
1 teaspoon Italian seasoning
½ teaspoon sea salt
Pepper to taste
Mushrooms (optional)
0 calorie sweetener of choice equal to 2 teaspoons sugar (optional)

Sauté meat until cooked; drain off fat. Add onion and garlic; sauté 2 to 3 minutes. Stir in all remaining ingredients. Cover pan; simmer for 20 minutes, stirring occasionally.   Simmer, uncovered for 20 minutes.

Yield: 12 servings   Serving Size: ¾ cup
Per Serving: Calories: 135; Fat: 3.0 g; Carb: 14.2 g; Dietary Fiber: 3.7 g; Sugar: 7.9 g; Protein: 13.1 g

Cook & Shopping Tip:

Low sugar and sugar free ketchup resources: This book has a ketchup recipe, Heinz has a low carb ketchup and Whole Foods and Trader Joe's usually carry sugar free ketchup.

Toppings (Breakfast and/or Dessert)

Berry Syrup

1 cup blueberries (fresh or frozen)
1 cup raspberries (fresh or frozen)
1 cup blackberries (fresh or frozen)
½ cup water
0 calorie sweetener of choice equal to ½ cup sugar
Pinch of salt

Combine all ingredients in a sauce pan and bring to a boil. Boil for 5 minutes. Turn off heat and mash berries with a fork to break them down. Boil for 2 additional minutes. Remove from heat. Syrup will thicken as it cools. Serve with pancakes, ice cream, and many other recipes in this book.

Yield: 1 ½ cups, 6 servings   Serving Size: ¼ cup
Per Serving: Calories: 35.0; Fat: 0.3 g; Carb: 10.3 g; Dietary Fiber: 3.2 g; Sugar: 4.5 g; Protein: 0.8 g

Peach Marmalade (Shown over cottage cheese)

5 cups crushed peaches
1 can crushed pineapple
1 large box of sugar free orange gelatin
0 calorie sweetener of choice equal to 7 cups sugar

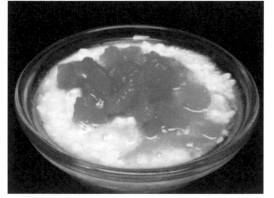

Cook the above ingredients for 15 minutes. When it reaches a rolling boil, add gelatin. Cook until dissolved. Pour in jars and seal or freeze.

Yield: 5 cups, approximately 36 servings
Serving Size: 2 tablespoons
Per Serving: Calories: 14.0; Fat: 0.1 g; Carb: 7.8 g; Dietary Fiber: 0.4 g; Sugar: 2.6 g; Protein: 0.4g

Chocolate Dipping Sauce

1 tablespoon virgin coconut oil
1½ tablespoons cocoa powder
0 calorie sweetener of choice to taste

Heat coconut oil, cocoa powder, and sweetener in a small sauce pan. Dip fruit and enjoy.

Variation: Dip different kinds of nuts and cool on wax paper. Store in refrigerator.

Yield: 1 serving
Per Serving: Calories: 73; Fat: 7.3 g; Carb: 3.2 g; Dietary Fiber: 1.2 g; Sugar: 1.1 g; Protein: 0.7 g

Soups

Oriental Beef Broccoli Soup

12 ounces broccoli, chopped
1 package Sun Bird Stir-fry seasoning
2 tablespoons soy sauce
0 calorie sweetener of choice equal to 2 teaspoons sugar
32 ounces beef broth
1 pound lean steak cut into squares, cooked

Combine all ingredients into a pan and simmer for 30 minutes.

Yield: 6 servings   Serving Size: 1 cup

Per Serving: Calories: 199; Fat: 5.8 g; Carb: 7.3 g; Dietary Fiber: 1.5 g; Sugar: 1.7 g; Protein 28.4 g

Buffalo Chicken Soup ⚠ CAUTION: High FAT

1 pound cooked chicken
⅓ cup Frank's Buffalo Sauce
1 can low fat cream of chicken soup
1 can low fat cream of mushroom soup
⅔ cup skim milk
⅔ cup low fat shredded cheddar cheese
3 ounce jar Hormel real bacon bits
3 ounces ⅓ less fat cream cheese

In a large sauce pan or crock pot, combine soups, milk, cheddar cheese and bacon and simmer. Cut up cooked chicken and add to the soup along with sauce. Simmer 15-20 minutes or until all is creamy and warm. You can add additional buffalo sauce to taste.

Yield: 6 servings   Serving Size: 1 cup
Per Serving: Calories: 300; Fat: 12.7 g; Carb: 10.3 g; Dietary Fiber: 0.9 g; Sugar: 2.8 g; Protein: 33.5 g

⚠ The caution sign identifies recipes that include caution items as ingredients. Some high fat caution items are milk, cheese, and nuts. Some high sugar (even though natural sugar) are pineapple and banana. Some high starchy vegetables are black beans and other legumes. These items are caution items for the 1st 3 weeks of maintenance. **Use these recipes in moderation and watch your morning weight closely, particularly during the 1st 3 weeks.**

Chicken Noodle Soup

2 cans chicken broth

4 (4 ounce) chicken breasts

1 (6 or 7 ounce) package Shirataki (fiber) Noodles*

¼ cup chopped onion

½ cup chopped celery

1 tablespoon Spike Vegetable Seasoning mix

1 (16 ounce) bag frozen vegetables (Optional)

*For best results when using Shirataki Noodles: Prior to use in a recipe, drain and thoroughly rinse the noodles with cold water. Place drained noodles in a non-stick frying pan and cook over medium heat, stirring occasionally, for approximately 10 minutes.

Cook chicken in chicken broth. Cool and cut into chunks. Add remaining ingredients and simmer for 30 minutes. Option: For Chicken Vegetable Noodle Soup, add vegetables.

Without vegetables option:
Yield: 4 servings   Serving Size: 1 cup
Per Serving Chicken Noodle Soup:
Calories: 235; Fat: 5.5 g; Carb: 2.9 g; Dietary Fiber: 0.4 g; Sugar: 1.3 g; Protein: 40.2 g
With vegetables option:
Yield: 4 servings   Serving Size: 1 ½ cups
Per Serving Chicken Vegetable Noodle Soup:
Calories: 303; Fat: 5.6 g; Carb: 17.7 g; Dietary Fiber: 5.4 g; Sugar: 4.8 g; Protein: 43.5 g

Clam Chowder – New England Style

⅔ cup mixture of onions and carrots (minced)

2 cups clam juice (may need to add water to bring to a cup)

2 sprigs parsley

2 bay leaves

8 ounces cooked clams (minced)

Pinch of thyme

White pepper to taste

Salt to taste

4 tablespoons heavy cream

In saucepan, sauté the onions and carrots in a bit of the clam juice until onions are clear. Add remaining clam juice, parsley and bay leaf. Simmer uncovered for 10 minutes. Add clams, thyme, pepper, salt and nonfat milk. Heat slowly and simmer for a few minutes. Remove bay leaf and parsley.

Yield: 2 servings   Serving Size: 1 cup
Per Serving: Calories: 288; Fat: 13.4 g; Carb: 10.6 g; Dietary Fiber: 1.0 g; Sugar: 1.7 g; Protein 46.1 g

Curry Cauliflower Soup

1 head cauliflower

1 chunked onion

3 halved cloves of garlic

5 cups vegetable stock

1 (14 ounce) can coconut milk

1 tablespoon curry paste

Preheat oven to 350° F. Rinse cauliflower and cut into florets. Place vegetables on cookie sheet and bake for 30 minutes until vegetables are golden brown. Heat vegetable stock, coconut milk and curry paste on high until boiling. Add roasted vegetables, cover and reduce heat to medium-low. Simmer for 15 minutes. Let cool down. Puree soup in a blender. Reheat and serve.

Yield: 8 servings   Serving Size: ¾ cup

Per Serving: Calories: 148; Fat: 14.2 g; Carb: 7.9 g; Dietary Fiber: 2.2 g; Sugar: 4.3 g; Protein: 2.1 g

> ⚠ The caution sign identifies recipes that include caution items as ingredients. Some high fat caution items are milk, cheese, and nuts. Some high sugar (even though natural sugar) are pineapple and banana. Some high starchy vegetables are black beans and other legumes. These items are caution items for the 1st 3 weeks of maintenance. **Use these recipes in moderation and watch your morning weight closely, particularly during the 1st 3 weeks.**

Italian Tomato Soup

1 pound chicken

2 cups water

2 (14.5 ounce) cans Hunts fire roasted tomatoes

1 can mushrooms

1 (14 ounce) can artichoke hearts, drained

¼ cup Classico Traditional Basil Pesto sauce, excess
     olive oil drained from top

Cook chicken with 2 cups of water to make broth. Set aside broth and cut chicken into small pieces. Drain and tear up artichoke hearts. Drain excess olive oil off top of pesto sauce. Add chicken pieces, tomatoes, mushrooms, artichoke hearts, and drained pesto to the chicken broth. Simmer for about 30 minutes.

Yield: 8 servings   Serving Size: 1 cup

Per Serving: Calories: 217; Fat: 6.8 g; Carb: 9.3 g; Dietary Fiber: 3.4 g; Sugar: 2.6 g; Protein 28.8 g

Sweet and Sour Soup

4 cups vegetable stock
1 cake firm tofu, cubed
4 slices fresh ginger root, ⅛ inch thick
½ teaspoon whole black peppercorn
3 large green onions, cut to 1 inch lengths
½ large sweet red pepper, seeded and sliced
½ cup fresh button mushrooms, sliced
¼ cup bamboo shoot
¼ cup rice wine vinegar
1 teaspoon chili powder
1 teaspoon sesame oil

In a large cooking pot, add chicken broth, sliced ginger root and peppercorns and bring to boil. Reduce heat to low and simmer uncovered for 20 minutes. Strain broth and discard ginger root and peppercorns. Return strained broth to cooking pot. Add sliced green onions, sliced red sweet pepper, sliced mushrooms, bamboo shoots, rice wine vinegar, chili powder and sesame oil. Bring to boil, reduce heat and simmer for 10 minutes or until vegetables are just tender crisp. Serve in soup bowls. If desired, serve this soup over cooked brown rice.

Yield: 8 servings   Serving Size: 1 cup
Per Serving: Calories: 61; Fat: 3.8 g; Carb: 4.1 g; Dietary Fiber: 1.3 g; Sugar: 2.2 g; Protein 4.7 g

> *Diet Tip:* Switch from soda to water or no-calorie iced tea to save major calories and cost.

Steak House French Onion Soup

1 (32 ounce) box beef broth
1 pound sirloin
2 chopped onions
2 cloves chopped garlic
2 tablespoons A1 steak sauce

Cook or grill sirloin and cut into 1 inch cubes. Combine cubes with other ingredients and simmer for 1 hour.

Yield: 6 servings   Serving Size: 1 cup
Per Serving: Calories: 173; Fat: 5.1 g; Carb: 4.8 g; Dietary Fiber: 0.6 g; Sugar: 2.2 g; Protein 25.2 g

Chinese Hot-and-Sour Soup

 5 ounces boneless pork loin, cut into ¼ inch thick strips (⅔ cup)

2 teaspoons dark soy sauce

4 small dried shitake mushrooms

2 tablespoons cornstarch

½ cup canned sliced bamboo shoots, cut lengthwise into ⅛ inch wide strips (from an 8 ounce can)

½ cup shredded carrots

4 tablespoons Chinese black vinegar

2 tablespoons rice vinegar (not seasoned)

1 tablespoon light soy sauce

0 calorie sweetener of choice equal to 1½ teaspoons sugar

1 teaspoon kosher sea salt

2 tablespoons peanut oil

4 cups reduced sodium chicken broth

4 ounces firm tofu (about a quarter of a block), rinsed and drained, then cut into ¼ inch thick strips

2 large eggs

2 teaspoons sesame oil

3 teaspoons freshly ground white pepper

2 tablespoons thinly sliced scallion greens

2 tablespoons fresh whole cilantro leaves

In a small bowl, toss pork with dark soy sauce until pork is well coated. Cover bamboo shoots with cold water by 2 inches in a small saucepan, and then bring just to a boil to remove bitterness. Drain in a sieve.   Stir together vinegars, light soy sauce, sweetener, and salt in another small bowl. Heat a wok over high heat until a bead of water vaporizes within 1 to 2 seconds of contact. Pour sesame oil down side of wok, and then swirl oil, tilting wok to coat sides. Add pork and stir-fry until meat just changes color, about 1 minute, then add mushrooms, bamboo shoots and carrots and stir-fry 1 minute.   Add broth and bring to a boil, then add tofu. Return to a boil and add vinegar mixture. Add water to cornstarch, then add to broth and return to a boil, stirring while mixture thickens. Reduce heat to medium and simmer 1 minute.   Beat eggs with a fork and add a few drops of sesame oil. Add eggs to soup in a thin stream, stirring slowly in one direction with a spoon. Stir in white pepper, then drizzle in remaining sesame oil and divide among bowls. Sprinkle with scallions and cilantro before serving.

Yield: 6 servings   Serving Size: 1 cup
Per Serving: Calories: 182; Fat: 10.2 g; Carb: 8.1 g; Dietary Fiber: 1.3 g; Sugar: 3.0 g; Protein 14.3 g

> **Shopping Tip:** A good source for uncommon cooking and baking ingredients is www.thecmccompany.com.

Taco Soup

2 pounds ground beef
¼ cup frozen corn
3 (14.5 ounce) cans Hunts fire roasted tomatoes
2 packets taco seasoning
12 ounce jar salsa
0 calorie sweetener equal to 1 tablespoon sugar
(Optional)

Brown ground beef and drain. In crock pot, combine all ingredients and simmer several hours.

Yield: 10 servings   Serving Size: 1 cup
Per Serving: Calories: 218; Fat: 6.9 g; Carb: 11.1 g; Dietary Fiber: 1.6 g; Sugar: 5.2 g; Protein 26.3g

Sides

Sweet Peas & Sun Dried Tomatoes

(Shown with Citrus Tilapia)

⅛ cup sun dried tomatoes
1 (12 ounce) bag sugar snap peas
1 tablespoon butter
Juice of ½ lemon
Sea salt & pepper to taste

Place all ingredients in a microwaveable bowl with a lid not quite closed. Steam for 5 minutes until peas are tender and serve.

Yield: 4 servings   Serving Size: ½ cup
Per Serving: Calories: 67; Fat: 3.2 g; Carb: 7.5 g; Dietary Fiber: 2.4 g; Sugar: 3.8 g; Protein: 2.5 g

Almond Broccoli

2 cups broccoli
¼ cup slivered almonds

Rinse broccoli, then grate or cut finely. Put in microwaveable dish and cook 4 – 5 minutes – do not add water. Add almonds.

Yield: 4 servings   Serving Size: ½ cup
Per Serving: Calories: 49; Fat: 3.1 g; Carb: 4.2 g; Dietary Fiber: 1.9 g; Sugar: 1.0 g; Protein: 2.5 g

Holiday Apple Cranberry Sauce

2 bags fresh cranberries
2 peeled apples cut in pieces
0 calorie sweetener of choice equal to 1½ cups sugar

Place berries and apples in pot. Cover with water and boil for approximately 20 minutes until apples are soft and berries have popped. Puree in a blender, and then put through a strainer. Stir in sweetener and refrigerate.

Yield: 12 servings   Serving Size: ½ cup
Per Serving: Calories: 47.0; Fat: 0.1 g; Carb: 13.9 g; Dietary Fiber: 4.0 g; Sugar: 5.4 g; Protein: 0.4 g

Mock Rice

½ head cauliflower

Rinse cauliflower, then grate or cut finely. Put in microwaveable dish and cook 4 – 5 minutes. Do not add water. Season as desired or use as rice in other recipes.

Yield: 4 servings   Serving Size: ½ cup
Per Serving: Calories: 8; Fat: 0.0 g; Carb: 1.8 g; Dietary Fiber: 0.8 g; Sugar: 0.8 g; Protein: 0.7 g

Wilted Spinach

(Shown with Chicken Parmesan)

1 bunch (about 10 ounces) whole fresh spinach leaves
3 tablespoons water
1 chicken bouillon cube
1 tablespoon butter
1 clove minced garlic
⅛ cup sun dried tomatoes (optional)

Dissolve bouillon cube in water. Remove stems and rinse well so that all leaves are moist. Place in a large pot, add bouillon, cover and heat on medium. When spinach begins to simmer, reduce heat to low and cook several minutes until leaves are just wilted. Transfer spinach to serving bowl. Press spinach with the back of spoon and pour off excess liquid. Cut through spinach a few times. Mix with garlic and tomatoes (optional). Top with butter and serve.

Yield: 2 servings
Per Serving: Calories: 105; Fat: 7.5 g; Carb: 7.7 g; Dietary Fiber: 3.6 g; Sugar: 0.9 g; Protein: 4.9 g

Creamy Cheese Noodles

1 cup low fat 2% cottage cheese
1 cup low fat sour cream
½ Vidalia onion, grated
1 teaspoon Worcestershire sauce
½ to ¾ teaspoon garlic salt
1 package Shirataki (fiber) Noodles*
1 cup Parmesan cheese, grated

*For best results when using Shirataki Noodles: Prior to use in a recipe, drain and thoroughly rinse the noodles with cold water. Place drained noodles in a non-stick frying pan and cook over medium heat, stirring occasionally, for approximately 10 minutes.

Preheat oven to 350° F. Mix together cottage cheese, sour cream, grated onion, Worcestershire sauce, and garlic salt. Stir in noodles. Prepare casserole dish with non stick cooking spray. Place mixture in prepared dish. Sprinkle top with grated Parmesan cheese. Bake for 45 minutes.

Yield: 6 servings   Serving Size ¾ cup
Per Serving: Calories: 168; Fat: 10.4 g; Carb: 5.5 g; Dietary Fiber: 0.2 g; Sugar: 1.0 g; Protein 12.9 g

Cheesy (Not) Potatoes

1 head cauliflower, chopped
1 can Campbell's Cream of Chicken & Mushroom Soup
¾ cup cheddar cheese
6 ounces ham, chopped (Optional)

Preheat oven to 350° F. Mix above & bake for 30 minutes or until cauliflower is tender.

Without Option:
Yield: 6 servings   Serving Size: ½ cup
Per Serving: Calories: 114; Fat: 7.7 g; Carb: 6.2 g;
Dietary Fiber: 1.1 g; Sugar: 1.4 g; Protein: 5.6 g

With Option:
Yield: 6 servings   Serving Size: ½ cup
Per Serving: Calories: 160; Fat: 10.1 g; Carb: 7.3 g; Dietary Fiber: 1.5 g; Sugar: 1.4 g; Protein: 10.3 g

---

⚠ The caution sign identifies recipes that include caution items as ingredients. Some high fat caution items are milk, cheese, and nuts. Some high sugar (even though natural sugar) are pineapple and banana. Some high starchy vegetables are black beans and other legumes. These items are caution items for the 1st 3 weeks of maintenance. **Use these recipes in moderation and watch your morning weight closely, particularly during the 1st 3 weeks.**

Broccoli Casserole

1 tablespoon olive oil

½ sliced onion

4 eggs

1 cup light mayonnaise

3 tablespoons almond flour (grind almonds in food processor)

1 teaspoon sea salt or to taste

½ teaspoon pepper or to taste

½ cup Parmesan cheese

2 (16 ounce) bags frozen chopped broccoli, thawed

Preheat oven to 375° F. Spray pie plate or 8" x 8" baking dish with non stick cooking spray. Heat oil in skillet over medium heat. Stir in onion, cook and stir until the onion is soft and translucent, about 5 minutes. Reduce heat to medium-low and continue to cook and stir until the onion is very tender and dark brown, 15 – 20 minutes. Set aside. Beat eggs with mayonnaise, flour, salt and pepper. Stir in cheese, broccoli and onion. Pour into prepared baking dish and bake until broccoli is tender, about 90 minutes. Divide into 8 slices.

Yield: 8 servings   Serving Size: 1 slice
Per Serving: Calories: 220; Fat: 16.4 g; Carb: 11.2 g; Dietary Fiber: 3.4 g; Sugar: 2.5 g; Protein: 9.0 g

> ⚠ The caution sign identifies recipes that include caution items as ingredients. Some high fat caution items are milk, cheese, and nuts. Some high sugar (even though natural sugar) are pineapple and banana. Some high starchy vegetables are black beans and other legumes. These items are caution items for the 1st 3 weeks of maintenance. **Use these recipes in moderation and watch your morning weight closely, particularly during the 1st 3 weeks.**

Mock Ranch Mashed Potatoes

1 head cauliflower
1 (8 ounce) package ⅓ less fat cream cheese
1 packet Ranch dressing mix

Rinse cauliflower and steam until tender, about 6 minutes. Place in a blender with cream cheese and dressing mix and blend until creamy. A mixer does not cream cauliflower enough.

Yield: 6 servings   Serving Size: ½ cup
Per Serving: Calories: 119; Fat: 8.1 g; Carb: 6.3 g; Dietary Fiber: 1.1 g; Sugar: 2.4 g; Protein: 3.8 g

Cranberry Nut Sauce

1 orange
12 ounces (3 cups) fresh or frozen cranberries
0 calorie sweetener of choice equal to 1 cup sugar
½ cup pecans

Peel orange, inspecting the skin for traces of pith, the bitter white inner skin, and cut off any that you find. Reserve the skin. Remove and discard the white pith from the orange and slice the fruit into sections, cutting off the separating membranes. Remove the seeds. Put the orange slices, the orange skin, pecans, and the cranberries into the bowl of a food processor fitted with a metal blade. Pulse 4 or 5 times or until the fruit is evenly chopped. Stir in sweetener until dissolved and refrigerate.

Yield: 6 servings   Serving Size: ¾ cup
Per Serving: Calories: 99; Fat: 6.6 g; Carb: 14.7 g; Dietary Fiber: 3.8 g; Sugar: 5.2 g; Protein: 1.3 g

> ⚠ The caution sign identifies recipes that include caution items as ingredients. Some high fat caution items are milk, cheese, and nuts. Some high sugar (even though natural sugar) are pineapple and banana. Some high starchy vegetables are black beans and other legumes. These items are caution items for the 1st 3 weeks of maintenance. **Use these recipes in moderation and watch your morning weight closely, particularly during the 1st 3 weeks.**

Butternut Squash Casserole

3 cups butternut squash, cooked and mashed
¼ cup skim milk
0 calorie sweetener of choice equal to 1 cup sugar
⅛ teaspoon nutmeg
Pinch of salt
1 teaspoon vanilla
2 eggs, lightly beaten
1 tablespoon melted butter
½ cup chopped pecans

Preheat oven to 350° F. Cut squash in half and remove seeds. Place squash, cut side down, in an ovenproof baking dish with about 1.2 inches of water. Bake about 1 hour until tender when pricked with a fork. Scoop out meat of squash and set aside. After cooled, blend squash and milk with an electric mixer until smooth. Add sweetener, nutmeg and salt, continuing to blend. Add eggs and vanilla continuing to blend. Transfer puree to an 8" x 8" non-stick ovenproof baking dish. Melt butter and toss pecans in it until coated. Sprinkle pecans over squash mixture and bake for 30 minutes.

Yield: 8 servings   Serving Size: ½ cup
Per Serving: Calories: 103; Fat: 7.5 g; Carb: 9.1 g; Dietary Fiber: 1.7 g; Sugar: 2.0 g; Protein: 2.8 g

Cabbage with Red Pepper Sauce

1 teaspoon coconut oil (or butter)
4 cups Chinese cabbage (sliced into ¼ inch diagonal
   pieces)
1 medium garlic clove, minced
1 pinch salt

Red Pepper Sauce:
8 ounces roasted peppers (jarred are fine)
1 teaspoon tamari (or Spike vegetable seasoning)

In heavy cast-iron skillet, heat coconut oil over high heat, then stir-fry Chinese cabbage and garlic with a pinch of salt until cabbage is wilted. Meanwhile, blend roasted red peppers in blender with tamari. Pour into saucepan and heat. To assemble, pile braised cabbage in serving dish and pour red pepper sauce over top. Serve immediately.

Yield: 4 servings   Serving Size: ¾ cup
Per Serving: Calories: 36; Fat: 1.4 g; Carb: 5.3 g; Dietary Fiber: 1.4 g; Sugar: 3.4 g; Protein: 1.8 g

Browned Vegetables

⅛ cup butter
⅛ cup olive oil
1 teaspoon garlic salt
1 teaspoon garlic pepper
2 tablespoons sliced almonds
2 tablespoons white wine
1 medium onion, chopped
1 medium red bell pepper, chopped
2 cups chopped broccoli
2 cups chopped cauliflower

Melt butter in a skillet over medium-low heat. Season with garlic salt and garlic pepper. Mix in almonds and cook until golden brown. Stir in wine, onion and red bell pepper, broccoli and cauliflower. Cook 5 minutes, or until vegetables are tender.

Yield: 6 servings   Serving Size: approximately ¾ cup
Per Serving: Calories: 123; Fat: 9.6 g; Carb: 7.8 g; Dietary Fiber: 2.7 g; Sugar: 3.1 g; Protein: 2.5 g

Lifestyle Tip: Change only one or two habits (or patterns) at a time. Perform each new habit until the new habit feels automatic, but for a minimum of 21 days. This is usually necessary to make sure the change (or new habit) is fully in effect.

Almond Broccoli with "Rice"
(Shown with Sun Dried Tomato Salmon)

1 head of cauliflower, grated
1 cup broccoli, chopped
3 tablespoons slivered almonds
1 teaspoon sea salt
Dash of pepper
1 tablespoon butter
Dash of Tony Chachere's Creole Seasoning

Mix the above ingredients, place in a microwave safe bowl with the lid slightly open. Steam for 5 minutes or until tender. Stir and serve.

Yield: 6 servings   Serving Size: ½ cup
Per Serving: Calories: 50; Fat: 3.5 g; Carb: 4.0 g; Dietary Fiber: 1.8 g; Sugar: 1.4 g; Protein: 1.9 g

> *Lifestyle Tip:* Exercise a few times each week.
> Try to do activities that you actually enjoy.

Pasta with Broccoli and Roasted Red Peppers

1 (6 or 7 ounce) package Shirataki (fiber) Noodles*
1 teaspoon olive oil
⅛ teaspoon hot pepper flakes
¼ cup water
1 cup broccoli florets
1 cup roasted peppers
¼ cup grated Parmesan cheese

*For best results when using Shirataki Noodles: Prior to use in a recipe, drain and thoroughly rinse the noodles with cold water. Place drained noodles in a non-stick frying pan and cook over medium heat, stirring occasionally, for approximately 10 minutes.

Warm oil and pepper flakes for about two minutes. Add broccoli and cook for 3 minutes. Add ¼ cup water, cover and cook until broccoli is tender-crisp, about 3 minutes. Toss in diced peppers. Toss prepared noodles with mixture and sprinkle with Parmesan cheese.

Yield: 6 servings   Serving Size: ½ cup
Per Serving: Calories: 61; Fat: 3.1 g; Carb: 5.4 g; Dietary Fiber: 1.1 g; Sugar: 2.5 g; Protein: 3.5 g

Parmesan Zucchini

1 zucchini cut lengthwise and about ¼ inch thick
1 egg
½ cup cheddar cheese
¼ teaspoon paprika
Dash of sea salt

Preheat oven to 350° F. Place zucchini on a cookie sheet. Mix the rest of the ingredients and spread on top of zucchini. Bake for 15 – 20 minutes until the cheese is melted and zucchini starts to get tender.

Yield: 4 servings   Serving Size: approximately 1 slice
Per Serving: Calories: 81; Fat: 5.9 g; Carb: 2.0 g; Dietary Fiber: 0.6 g; Sugar: 1.0 g; Protein: 5.5 g

Creamed Spinach

5 tablespoons butter

¼ cup almond flour

½ teaspoon sea salt

¼ teaspoon black pepper

1 dash ground nutmeg

1 cup half and half cream

4 ounces ⅓ less fat cream cheese

1 small onion - minced

3 cloves garlic - minced

2 (10 ounce) packages frozen chopped spinach - thawed and drained

¼ cup water

¼ cup grated Asiago or Parmesan cheese

In 2 quart pan, medium-low heat, melt 3 tablespoons butter; stir in flour, salt, pepper, and nutmeg; slowly whisk in cream; stir in cream cheese. Increase heat to medium; whisk mixture constantly until thick and smooth; remove from heat and set aside. In a skillet over medium-high heat, cook onions and garlic in remaining 2 tablespoons butter; stir spinach and water into pan. Reduce heat to medium-low; cover; simmer, stirring occasionally, for 8 minutes. Stir spinach mixture into creamy mixture; return to medium heat; stirring often, until warmed. Remove from heat; fold in Parmesan.

Yield: 8 servings   Serving Size: ½ cup
Per Serving: Calories: 190; Fat: 16.5 g; Carb: 6.3 g; Dietary Fiber: 2.1 g; Sugar: 1.4 g; Protein: 5.7 g

> ⚠ The caution sign identifies recipes that include caution items as ingredients. Some high fat caution items are milk, cheese, and nuts. Some high sugar (even though natural sugar) are pineapple and banana. Some high starchy vegetables are black beans and other legumes. These items are caution items for the 1st 3 weeks of maintenance. **Use these recipes in moderation and watch your morning weight closely, particularly during the 1st 3 weeks.**

Green Beans with Sun Dried Tomatoes

1 (16 ounce) package French green beans
1 cup sun dried tomatoes
1 tablespoon butter
Sea salt and pepper to taste

Cook green beans according to package instructions. Add butter, tomatoes, salt and pepper.

Yield: 5 servings   Serving Size: ¾ cup
Per Serving: Calories: 81; Fat: 3.6 g; Carb: 11.1 g; Dietary Fiber: 3.9 g; Sugar: 3.3 g; Protein: 2.5 g

Lemon Pepper Snap Peas

1 package frozen snap peas
1 teaspoon butter
1 teaspoon lemon pepper seasoning

Place peas in microwaveable steamer. Steam for 4 minutes. Add butter and seasoning and serve.

Yield: 4 servings   Serving Size: ½ cup
Per Serving: Calories: 44; Fat: 1.1; Carb: 6.4 g; Dietary Fiber: 2.2 g; Sugar: 3.4 g; Protein: 2.4 g

Mock Hash Browns

½ head cauliflower
3 slices chopped bacon
½ cup chopped onion
2 teaspoons butter
½ teaspoon salt or to taste
¼ teaspoon pepper or to taste

Rinse cauliflower and then grate. Fry bacon and onion until both start to brown. Add grated cauliflower. Cook and stir until the cauliflower is browned and tender. Add butter occasionally to assist with the browning. Season with salt and pepper.

Yield: 4 servings   Serving Size: ½ cup
Per Serving: Calories: 57; Fat: 3.9 g; Carb: 3.2 g; Dietary Fiber: 1.1 g; Sugar: 1.4 g; Protein: 2.6 g

Sugar Snap Peas
(Shown as bedding)

2 cups fresh sugar snap peas
1 tablespoon olive oil (or 2 teaspoons olive and 1 teaspoon sesame oil for extra flavor)
2 teaspoons scallions, minced
½ teaspoon garlic, minced
1 teaspoon chopped fresh thyme (optional)
½ teaspoon Kosher salt or to taste

Preheat oven to 450° F. Remove the stem ends and string down the side of the pea pods. Place all ingredients in a bowl and toss to coat. Spread sugar snap peas in a single layer on a medium baking sheet.   In the preheated oven, bake 6 – 10 minutes depending on preference of tenderness versus crispy.

Yield: 4 servings   Serving Size: ½ cup
Per Serving: Calories: 45; Fat: 3.5 g; Carb: 2.7 g; Dietary Fiber: 1.0 g; Sugar: 1.3 g; Protein: 0.9 g

---

Healthy Tip: Drink lots of plain water every day.

Protein Spinach Bake

1 (10 ounce) package frozen spinach
2 tablespoons chopped Vidalia or sweet onion
1 teaspoon minced garlic
1 ¼ cups low fat 2% cottage cheese
⅛ teaspoon rosemary
¼ teaspoon oregano
2 teaspoons Parmesan cheese

Preheat oven to 350° F. Spray a small baking dish with non-stick cooking spray. Cook spinach, garlic and onion in a pan with a bit of water until the onion is soft and the spinach is thawed. Squeeze water out and spread in bottom of baking dish. Mix cottage cheese with rosemary and oregano and spread over spinach. Sprinkle with Parmesan cheese.   Bake 25 – 30 minutes until cheese is bubbling.

Yield: 4 servings   Serving Size: ½ cup
Per Serving: Calories: 96; Fat: 2.3 g; Carb: 7.0 g; Dietary Fiber: 2.9 g; Sugar: 0 .8 g; Protein: 13.0 g

Spanish "Rice"

1 head cauliflower, shredded
½ pound lean sausage
1 cup salsa
1 green pepper chopped
½ onion chopped
4 slices Monterey Jack with Jalapeño Pepper Cheese

Brown sausage and drain drippings. Brown onion and peppers. Add salsa and cauliflower. Cook until cauliflower is tender (15 minutes). Add cheese and stir.

Yield: 6 servings   Serving Size: ⅔ cup
Per Serving: Calories: 159; Fat: 8.1 g; Carb: 9.2 g; Dietary Fiber: 2.3 g; Sugar: 3.4 g; Protein: 12.8 g

Spaghetti Squash

1 spaghetti squash or 4 cups spaghetti squash
Water
Sea salt or garlic salt

Preheat oven to 350° F. Spaghetti squash is a great substitute for pasta. Cut spaghetti squash in halves or quarters, lengthwise. Scrape out seeds. Place squash, cut side down in a baking pan with about ½ inch of water. Bake for 45 – 60 minutes, depending on size, until tender when pricked with a fork. To boil, place in a pan with a couple inches of water and cook for about 20 minutes. Let squash cool slightly. Remove and separate strands by running a fork through in the "stem to stern" direction. Add seasoning of your choice or use as 'spaghetti noodles' in other recipes.

Yield: 4 servings   Serving Size: 1 cup
Per Serving: Calories: 42; Fat: 0.4 g; Carb: 10.0 g; Dietary Fiber: 2.2 g; Sugar: 3.9 g; Protein: 1.0 g

Cabbage & Turkey Bacon

1 head of cabbage, chopped
¼ cup water
½ pound turkey bacon, sliced bite-sized
1 Vidalia onion, chopped
1 teaspoon salt or to taste
½ teaspoon pepper or to taste

In a skillet, cook cut bacon until crisp. Remove bacon from the pan. Add butter and sauté the onion. Add water, salt, and pepper until dissolved. Add cut cabbage; cover and steam for 10 – 15 minutes until cabbage is tender, stirring often. Add salt and pepper to taste.

Yield: 6 servings   Serving Size: ⅔ cup
Per Serving: Calories: 87; Fat: 1.4 g; Carb: 8.6 g; Dietary Fiber: 3.3 g; Sugar: 4.6 g; Protein: 9.3 g

Creamy Fruit Salad

¾ cup heavy cream whipped
0 calorie sweetener equal to 2 teaspoons sugar
⅓ cup light mayonnaise
¼ cup grapes, halved and seeded
1 cup diced apples
1 cup sliced strawberries
1 cup sliced peaches

Blend cream, sweetener and mayonnaise. Fold in remaining ingredients. Chill.

Yield: 4 servings   Serving Size: approximately ¾ cup
Per Serving: Calories: 184; Fat: 14.6 g; Carb: 13.8 g; Dietary Fiber: 2.1 g; Sugar: 9.1 g; Protein: 1.2 g

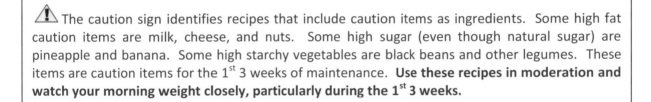

⚠ The caution sign identifies recipes that include caution items as ingredients. Some high fat caution items are milk, cheese, and nuts. Some high sugar (even though natural sugar) are pineapple and banana. Some high starchy vegetables are black beans and other legumes. These items are caution items for the 1st 3 weeks of maintenance. **Use these recipes in moderation and watch your morning weight closely, particularly during the 1st 3 weeks.**

Snacks

Quick, handy ideas for snacks that you can pick up and go:

Fruits
Vegetables
Edamame (young soybeans)
Celery with cheese* or peanut butter*
Apple with peanut butter*
Cottage cheese with real fruit
Jerky (most flavors, but watch the sugars)
Pork Rinds
Venison/deer jerky
Almonds*
Peanuts*

Cheese cubes/sticks*
Celery filled with tuna or chicken salad

Dessert-like Snacks
Sugar-free fat-free Jell-O
Sugar-free fat-free pudding
Berries with fat-free milk or cream
Strawberries with Brie cheese*
Skinny Cow Skinny Dippers*
Sugary pecans (dessert section)
Sweet roasted walnuts (dessert section)

*These items are caution items for the 1st 3 weeks of maintenance. Eat these in moderation and watch your morning weight closely.

Other convenient combination food snacks i.e. snack bars, yogurts, trail mixes, etc.* may work well for you in moderation, while some may not, as people and metabolism combinations vary significantly. Combination foods that make good, healthy snacks generally should have Carbohydrates - 15 or less, Fiber - 2 or more, Sugar - 10 or less, and Protein - 4 or more. Some of the higher sugar examples below made the list because some of the 'sugar' is from the real fruit in the snack, so it is different than processed sugar.

Note: The less carbs/sugar grams, the better. The more fiber/protein grams, the better.

Pure Protein Bar – Chocolate Peanut Butter* (Avg.: Carb 16 g, Fiber 1 g, Sugar 2 g, Protein 20 g)*
True North Pecan Almond Peanut Clusters* (Carb 9 g, Fiber 2 g, Sugar 5 g, Protein, 5 g)*
Planters Trail Mix Energy Mix* (Carb 14 g, Fiber 3 g, Sugar 6 g, Protein 6 g)*
Slim Fast High Protein – Peanut Granola* (Carb 20 g, Fiber 2 g, Sugar 10 g*, Protein 15 g) – Caution*
Ksar Pistachios – Sahale Snacks Nut Blend* (Carb 11 g, Fiber 3 g, Sugar 3 g, Protein 5 g)*
Trader Joe's Organic Almonds, Cashews & Cranberries* (Carb 15 g, Fiber 5 g, Sugar 8 g, Protein 9 g)*
Trader Joe's – San Wasabi Peas* (Carb 19 g, Fiber 1 g, Sugar 2 g, Protein 4 g)*
GREEK plain yogurt* (Carb 6 – 9 g, Fiber 1 g, Sugar 6 g, Protein 18 g)
Dannon Light & Fit Carb & Sugar Control* (Carb 3 g, Fiber 0 g, Sugar 2 g, Protein 5 g)*
Fiber One Creamy Non-Fat Yogurt* (Carb 19 g, Fiber 5 g, Sugar 11 g, Protein 4 g)*
Trio bars* (Carb 14 g, Fiber 2 g, Sugar 6 g, Protein 5 g)*

*These items are caution items for the 1st 3 weeks of maintenance. Eat these in moderation and watch your morning weight closely.

Desserts

Popsicles

1 package sugar free Kool-Aid, any flavor
1 small package sugar free Jell-O
1 cup hot water
0 calorie sweetener of choice equal to 1 cup sugar
1½ cups cold water

Dissolve Kool-Aid, Jell-O and sweetener in hot water. Add cold water. Pour into popsicle mold and freeze for 8 hours.

Yield: 12   Serving Size: 1 popsicle
Per Serving: Calories: 3; Fat: 0.0 g; Carb: 2.7 g; Dietary Fiber: 0.0 g; Sugar: 0.0 g; Protein: 0.2 g

Fudgesicles

(Shown with Berry Popsicle)

4 tablespoons fat free, sugar-free instant Jell-O Chocolate
    pudding
0 calorie sweetener of choice equal to 2 tablespoons sugar
1 egg
Pinch of salt
1 teaspoon vanilla
1½ cups 2% milk

Mix all ingredients thoroughly. Pour into popsicle mold. Freeze for eight hours.

Yield: 8   Serving Size: 1 fudgesicle
Per Serving: Calories: 44; Fat: 1.5 g; Carb: 5.7 g; Dietary Fiber: 0.3 g; Sugar: 2.3 g; Protein: 2.3 g

Crustless Cheesecake

16 ounces cream cheese
2 eggs
2 teaspoons vanilla
16 ounces sour cream
2 tablespoons melted butter
1/2 cup Malitol syrup (can also use sweetener or sugar free syrup)

Preheat oven to 325° F. Beat all ingredients together. Pour into a spring form pan. Bake for 30-40 minutes. When time is up, turn off the oven, BUT don't take the cake out. Let it cool completely before opening the oven door. Refrigerate.

Yield: 10 servings

Per Serving: Calories: 272; Fat: 26.2 g; Carb: 4.3 g; Dietary Fiber: 0.0; Sugar: 0.3 g; Protein: 5.6 g

Strawberry Pie

Crust:
¾ cup almond meal
2 tablespoons butter
0 calorie sweetener equal to 2 tablespoons sugar

Preheat oven to 325° F. Combine ingredients for crust and press into bottom of pan. Bake for 7 – 10 minutes until beginning to brown. Cool.

Filling:
1 pint strawberries cut in half
1 tablespoon cornstarch
1 cup hot water
1 small package strawberry sugar free Jell-O (3 tablespoons dry mix)
0 calorie sweetener of choice equal to 1 cup sugar

Put berries in baked shell. Cook sweetener, water and cornstarch until thick. Remove from heat; add Jell-O and stir well. Cool, then pour over strawberries. Top with whipped topping. Cut into 8 slices.

Yield: 8 servings   Serving Size: 1 slice

Per Serving: Calories: 146; Fat: 12.0 g; Carb: 11.4 g; Dietary Fiber: 2.2 g; Sugar: 3.4 g; Protein: 3.3 g

---

⚠ The caution sign identifies recipes that include caution items as ingredients. Some high fat caution items are milk, cheese, and nuts. Some high sugar (even though natural sugar) are pineapple and banana. Some high starchy vegetables are black beans and other legumes. These items are caution items for the 1st 3 weeks of maintenance. **Use these recipes in moderation and watch your morning weight closely, particularly during the 1st 3 weeks.**

Yogurt Jello Dessert

1 small package sugar free gelatin, any flavor
8 ounces hot water
16 ounces 2% Greek yogurt

Boil water, add gelatin and stir until completely dissolved. Let chill until not warm. Blend in 16 ounces plain Greek yogurt. Chill to set.

Yield: 4 servings   Serving Size: ½ cup
Per Serving: Calories: 76; Fat: 2.3 g; Carb: 4.5 g; Dietary Fiber: 0.0 g; Sugar: 4.5 g; Protein: 10.0 g

Baked Pear

2 Bartlett pears
2 teaspoons cinnamon
1 cup fresh raspberries (frozen will suffice)
1 (4 ounce) container of Fiber One Vanilla Yogurt
2 teaspoons sugar free maple syrup

Preheat oven to 350° F. Cut pears in half, remove core and place in a 9" x 9" baking dish. Dash the top of the pears with about ½ teaspoon cinnamon. In the cored area of the pear, put about 5 berries and bake for about 20 minutes. Remove from oven and cool slightly. Serve warm with 2 tablespoons of yogurt dolloped on each pear half. Drizzle with ½ teaspoon sugar free maple syrup and garnish with remaining raspberries.

Yield: 4 servings   Serving Size: ½ pear
Per Serving: Calories: 93; Fat: 0.3 g; Carb: 24.5 g; Dietary Fiber: 7.1 g; Sugar: 13.1 g; Protein: 1.6 g

Strawberry Fluff

1 large package sugar free strawberry gelatin
1 pound frozen sliced strawberries
1 (8 ounce) Cool Whip

Prepare gelatin per directions on the package and add crushed strawberries. Refrigerate until slightly thickened. Beat in Cool Whip with electric mixer until well mixed. Refrigerate until set.

Yield: 8 servings   Serving Size: approximately ⅔ cup
Per Serving: Calories: 41; Fat: 0.9 g; Carb: 7.7 g; Dietary Fiber: 0.8 g; Sugar: 4.6 g; Protein: 0.8 g

Fruit Pizza

Crust:

¾ cup almond meal

2 tablespoons butter

0 calorie sweetener of choice equal to 2 tablespoons sugar

Preheat oven to 325° F. Combine ingredients for crust. Press and bake on a flat round cookie sheet. Bake for 7 – 10 minutes until beginning to brown. Remove from oven and let cool.

Topping:

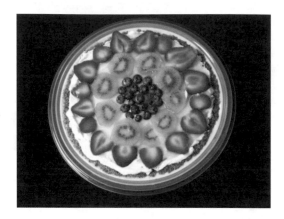

1 (8 ounce) package low fat cream cheese, softened

1 (8 ounce) container frozen whipped topping, thawed

2 cups sliced fresh strawberries

2 – 3 kiwis, peeled and sliced

2 cups blueberries

0 calorie sweetener of choice equal to 2 tablespoons sugar

1 tablespoon cornstarch

Juice of one medium orange (1 ounce)

2 tablespoons lemon juice

¼ cup water

½ teaspoon orange zest

In a large bowl, soften cream cheese, and then fold in the whipped topping. Spread over cooled crust. You can chill for a while at this point or continue by arranging the fruit. Begin with strawberries, sliced in half. Arrange in a circle around the outside edge. Continue to layer fruit in circles moving inward. In a saucepan, combine sweetener, salt, corn starch, orange juice, lemon juice and water. Cook and stir this sauce over medium heat. Bring the sauce to a boil and cook for 1 or 2 minutes until thickened. Remove from heat and add grated orange rind.   Allow to cool but not set. Spoon the cooled sauce over the fruit. Chill for two hours; cut into 12 wedges and serve.

Yield: 12 servings   Serving Size: 1 slice
Per Serving: Calories: 192; Fat: 14.3 g; Carb: 14.3 g; Dietary Fiber: 2.4; Sugar: 7.5 g; Protein: 4.2 g

---

⚠ The caution sign identifies recipes that include caution items as ingredients. Some high fat caution items are milk, cheese, and nuts. Some high sugar (even though natural sugar) are pineapple and banana. Some high starchy vegetables are black beans and other legumes. These items are caution items for the 1st 3 weeks of maintenance. **Use these recipes in moderation and watch your morning weight closely, particularly during the 1st 3 weeks.**

Pineapple Delight

CAUTION: High Sugar

1 small box sugar free, fat free vanilla pudding
2 cups skim milk
½ can crushed pineapple in its own juice
1 (20 ounce) can chunk pineapple, drained, no sugar
½ tub light cool whip

Make sugar free, fat free pudding as directed on box. After pudding is chilled, add other ingredients and mix together.

Yield: 8 servings   Serving Size: ½ cup
Per Serving: Calories: 121; Fat: 1.7 g; Carb: 24.6 g; Dietary Fiber: 1.2 g; Sugar: 16.6 g; Protein: 2.6 g

Ice Cream

CAUTION: High FAT

You will need a 1 ½ quart ice cream maker i.e. the Cuisinart with the core that is kept in your freezer works well.

1 ⅛ cups Unsweetened Almond Breeze Vanilla Milk
1 ⅛ cups Malitol Syrup (available from Joseph's Lites@www.josephslitecookies.com)
2¼ cups heavy whipping cream
1 tablespoon vanilla
Pinch of cinnamon (Optional)

In medium mixing bowl, combine all of the ingredients. Turn on the ice cream maker. Pour the mixture through the top of the lid. Let mix until thickened, about 20-25 minutes. This will be ready to eat in a soft/creamy texture. If you prefer the dessert to have a thicker consistency, transfer the mixture to a covered container and freeze for 2 hours.

Yield: 8 servings   Serving Size ½ cup
Per Serving: Calories: 147; Fat: 12.9 g; Carb: 8.2 g; Dietary Fiber: 0.0; Sugar: 7.0 g; Protein: 0.8 g

Tasty Tip: Fresh fruit and other additives would taste delicious with this ice cream, so be imaginative, but use caution with amounts and watch your next morning weight.

⚠ The caution sign identifies recipes that include caution items as ingredients. Some high fat caution items are milk, cheese, and nuts. Some high sugar (even though natural sugar) are pineapple and banana. Some high starchy vegetables are black beans and other legumes. These items are caution items for the 1st 3 weeks of maintenance. **Use these recipes in moderation and watch your morning weight closely, particularly during the 1st 3 weeks.**

Sweet Roasted Walnuts

1 tablespoon butter
1 ½ cups walnuts
1 tablespoon sugar free maple syrup
0 calorie sweetener of choice equal to 2 tablespoons sugar

Preheat oven to 250° F. Melt butter, add syrup, and sweetener. Roll walnuts into mixture until coated. Place single layer on baking sheet and bake for 15 – 20 minutes. Be careful not to let them burn. Remove from oven and spread on a cookie sheet to dry. Add sweetener of choice when they are warm (not hot) for a "crystallized" effect.

Yield: 12 servings   Serving Size: 2 tablespoons
Per Serving: Calories: 106; Fat: 10.2 g; Carb: 2.1 g; Dietary Fiber: 1.1 g; Sugar: .4 g; Protein: 3.8 g

Caramel Pecan Cheesecake Flan

6 ounces cream cheese
½ cup part-skim ricotta cheese
0 calorie sweetener of choice equal to 3 tablespoons sugar
1 large egg
1 large egg yolk
½ teaspoon vanilla
2 tablespoons sugar free caramel sundae sauce
2 tablespoons sugar free maple syrup
2 tablespoons chopped pecans

Preheat oven to 350° F. Sit cheeses out until they reach room temperature. Cream cheeses together. Blend in next four ingredients until creamy. Pour into a flan pan. Mix sundae sauce, syrup and pecans and pour over top. Use a knife to make a swirl pattern. Place the flan in a pan filled with ½" water. Bake about 30 minutes until set. Chill for at least 2 hours. Divide into 6 slices.

Yield: 6 servings   Per Serving: 1 slice
Per Serving: Calories: 183; Fat: 14.7 g; Carb: 7.5 g; Dietary Fiber: 0.0 g; Sugar: 0.0 g; Protein: 6.2 g

---

⚠ The caution sign identifies recipes that include caution items as ingredients. Some high fat caution items are milk, cheese, and nuts. Some high sugar (even though natural sugar) are pineapple and banana. Some high starchy vegetables are black beans and other legumes. These items are caution items for the 1st 3 weeks of maintenance. **Use these recipes in moderation and watch your morning weight closely, particularly during the 1st 3 weeks.**

Sugary Pecans

1 pound pecans
1 egg white
1 tablespoon water

Sugar Mix:
0 calorie sweetener of choice equal to 1 cup sugar
1 teaspoon salt
1 teaspoon cinnamon

Preheat oven to 300° F. In a small bowl, combine sweetener, salt and cinnamon and set aside. Beat egg white and water until frothy. Toss the nuts with the egg white mix. Then toss in the sugar mix. Bake on a cookie sheet for 30 minutes. Stir after 15 minutes.

Yield: 16 servings   Serving Size: 1 ounce
Per Serving: Calories: 197.0; Fat: 20.4 g; Carb: 5.6 g; Dietary Fiber: 2.8 g; Sugar: 1.1 g; Protein: 2.8 g

Chocolate Pecan Torte

2 cups pecans
⅓ cup cocoa
1 teaspoon baking powder
¼ teaspoon salt
5 eggs
½ cup melted butter
1 teaspoon vanilla
0 calorie sweetener of choice equal to 1 cup sugar
½ cup water

Preheat oven to 350° F. Pulse pecans in food processor until like meal, although they won't get quite as small as corn meal. Add remainder of dry ingredients and continue to pulse. Add wet ingredients and process until blended well. Pour into greased 8" or 9" round pan or spring form pan. Baking time will vary depending on pan used. Begin checking after 25 minutes. Torte is done when toothpick inserted in the center comes out clean. Cut into 10 slices.

Yield: 10 servings   Serving Size: 1 slice
Per Serving: Calories: 282; Fat: 27.3 g; Carb: 7.4 g; Dietary Fiber: 2.9 g; Sugar: 3.5 g; Protein: 5.4 g

⚠ The caution sign identifies recipes that include caution items as ingredients. Some high fat caution items are milk, cheese, and nuts. Some high sugar (even though natural sugar) are pineapple and banana. Some high starchy vegetables are black beans and other legumes. These items are caution items for the 1st 3 weeks of maintenance. **Use these recipes in moderation and watch your morning weight closely, particularly during the 1st 3 weeks.**

Pumpkin Cheesecake

CAUTION: High FAT

Crust:

¾ cup almond meal

¼ cup finely chopped pecans

2 tablespoons melted butter

0 calorie sweetener of choice equal to 2 tablespoons sugar

Filling:

2 (8 ounce) packages cream cheese (room temperature)

1 can pumpkin

4 eggs (room temperature)

1½ teaspoons vanilla

1 teaspoon cinnamon

1 teaspoon nutmeg

¼ teaspoon ginger

¼ teaspoon cloves

0 calorie sweetener of choice equal to 1 ⅓ cups sugar

¼ cup sour cream

Preheat oven to 325° F. Combine ingredients for crust and press into bottom of spring form pan. Bake for 8-10 minutes until beginning to brown. Remove and set aside to cool. Beat room temperature cream cheese until fluffy. Add other ingredients, continuously scraping the bowl and beaters until each ingredient is fully incorporated. After all ingredients are combined, scrape bowl one last time and beat one minute.

Wrap the sides and bottom of the spring form pan in tin foil. Pour filling mixture over crust in pan. Place it in a baking pan and pour boiling water into the baking pan so that the spring form pan is surrounded. Bake at 350 for 60 – 90 minutes. Check often. Cake is done when it is slightly soft in the center but firm to the touch. Divide into 12 slices.

Yield: 12 servings   Serving Size: 1 slice
Per Serving: Calories: 245; Fat: 22.3 g; Carb: 9.1 g; Dietary Fiber: 2.1 g; Sugar: 1.8 g; Protein: 6.8 g

---

⚠ The caution sign identifies recipes that include caution items as ingredients. Some high fat caution items are milk, cheese, and nuts. Some high sugar (even though natural sugar) are pineapple and banana. Some high starchy vegetables are black beans and other legumes. These items are caution items for the 1st 3 weeks of maintenance. **Use these recipes in moderation and watch your morning weight closely, particularly during the 1st 3 weeks.**

Tasty Tip: This cheesecake recipe can be used with several crust recipes in this book – just remember to take the nutritional value of the crust into consideration.

Strawberry Cheesecake

Crust:

1 cup almond meal
2 tablespoons melted butter
0 calorie sweetener of choice equal to 2 tablespoons sugar

Filling:

3 (8 ounce) packages cream cheese (room temperature)
4 eggs (room temperature)
1½ teaspoons vanilla
Juice squeezed from ½ lemon
0 calorie sweetener of choice equal to 1 ⅓ cups sugar
¼ cup sour cream

Strawberry Topping:

2 cups chopped fresh strawberries
0 calorie sweetener of choice equal to ½ cup sugar

Preheat oven to 325° F. Combine ingredients for crust and press into bottom of spring form pan. Bake for 8-10 minutes until beginning to brown. Remove and set aside to cool. Beat room temperature cream cheese until fluffy. Add other ingredients, continuously scraping the bowl and beaters until each ingredient is fully incorporated. After all ingredients are combined, scrape bowl one last time and beat one minute.

Wrap the sides and bottom of the spring form pan in tin foil. Pour filling mixture over crust in pan. Place it in a baking pan and pour boiling water into the baking pan so that the spring form pan is surrounded. Bake at 350° F for 60 – 90 minutes. Check often. Cake is done when it is slightly soft in the center but firm to the touch.

Prepare strawberry topping by chopping strawberries and adding sweetener. Keep topping separate until ready to serve. When ready to serve, divide cheesecake into 12 slices, place each slice on serving dish, and top with 2 tablespoons of the topping.

Yield: 12 servings   Serving Size: 1 slice plus 2 tablespoons of topping
Per Serving: Calories: 311; Fat: 29.1 g; Carb: 10.0 g; Dietary Fiber: 1.5 g; Sugar: 1.8 g; Protein: 8.3 g

⚠ The caution sign identifies recipes that include caution items as ingredients. Some high fat caution items are milk, cheese, and nuts. Some high sugar (even though natural sugar) are pineapple and banana. Some high starchy vegetables are black beans and other legumes. These items are caution items for the 1st 3 weeks of maintenance. **Use these recipes in moderation and watch your morning weight closely, particularly during the 1st 3 weeks.**

Cooking Tip: When baking cheesecake, it helps to put a pan of water in the oven on the same shelf or wrap the pan in foil and place in a water bath.

Iced Berry Salad

CAUTION: High FAT

0 calorie sweetener of choice equal to ¾ cup sugar

8 ounces sour cream

1 tablespoon grated lemon peel

2 tablespoons lemon juice

1 cup whipping cream

1 teaspoon vanilla

1 cup strawberries (may use frozen)

1 cup blueberries (may use frozen)

1 cup raspberries (may use frozen)

Combine sweetener alternate, sour cream, lemon juice and lemon peel. In chilled small mixing bowl, beat chilled whipping cream at high speed. Scrape bowl often and beat 1-2 minutes until stiff peaks form. Fold whipped cream, vanilla and berries into sour cream mixture by hand. Pour mixture into loaf pan lined with foil. Freeze 6 hours or overnight. Lift salad from pan and remove foil. Slice into eight 1 inch slices and serve frozen.

Yield: 8 servings   Serving Size: ½ cup
Per Serving: Calories: 131; Fat: 10.8 g; Carb: 10.3 g; Dietary Fiber: 1.9 g; Sugar: 3.6 g; Protein: 1.7 g

> ⚠ The caution sign identifies recipes that include caution items as ingredients. Some high fat caution items are milk, cheese, and nuts. Some high sugar (even though natural sugar) are pineapple and banana. Some high starchy vegetables are black beans and other legumes. These items are caution items for the 1st 3 weeks of maintenance. **Use these recipes in moderation and watch your morning weight closely, particularly during the 1st 3 weeks.**

Strawberry Parfait

4 ounces 2% fat Greek yogurt with 0 calorie sweetener of choice equal to 2 teaspoons sugar, mixed

6 large strawberries

0 calorie sweetener of choice equal to 1 teaspoon sugar

Slice strawberries and add sweetener. Layer the strawberries and yogurt.

Yield: 1 serving
Per Serving: Calories: 97; Fat: 2.5 g; Carb: 11.1 g; Dietary Fiber: 1.4 g; Sugar: 8.1 g; Protein: 10.1 g

Fluffy Peanut Butter Dip

½ cup creamy peanut butter

8 ounces Greek yogurt

0 calorie sweetener equal to 1 tablespoon sugar or to taste

⅛ teaspoon cinnamon

½ cup thawed sugar free whipped topping

Mix yogurt with sweetener and cinnamon. Cream in peanut butter and lightly fold in whipped topping. Chill for one hour. Serve with fresh fruit for dipping.

Yield: 8 servings   Serving Size: ¼ cup

Per Serving: Calories: 129; Fat: 9.5 g; Carb: 6.8 g; Dietary Fiber: 1.0 g; Sugar: 2.6 g; Protein: 6.5 g

Peanut Butter Cookies

0 calorie sweetener of choice equal to ¾ cup sugar

1 large egg

1 teaspoon vanilla

1 cup creamy peanut butter

1 teaspoon baking soda

Preheat oven to 350° F. Line a cookie sheet with parchment paper. Beat sweetener, egg and vanilla with a mixer for 3 minutes on low. Add baking soda and peanut butter and mix on medium for about 30 seconds. Scoop balls of dough with a teaspoon and roll in sweetener. Divide into 12 balls. Place on cookie sheet about an inch apart. Press with a fork to make a tic-tac-toe pattern. Bake about 13 minutes until lightly browned on the bottom. Cool on wire rack.

Yield: 12 servings   Serving Size: approximately 1 cookie

Per Serving: Calories: 133; Fat: 11.2 g; Carb: 5.8 g; Dietary Fiber: 1.3 g; Sugar: 2.0 g; Protein: 5.9 g

---

The caution sign identifies recipes that include caution items as ingredients. Some high fat caution items are milk, cheese, and nuts. Some high sugar (even though natural sugar) are pineapple and banana. Some high starchy vegetables are black beans and other legumes. These items are caution items for the 1st 3 weeks of maintenance. **Use these recipes in moderation and watch your morning weight closely, particularly during the 1st 3 weeks.**

Peanut Butter Pie

Crust:
¾ cup crushed peanuts or ¾ cup almond meal
¼ cup finely chopped pecans
2 tablespoons melted butter
0 calorie sweetener of choice equal to 2 tablespoons sugar

Filling:
1 cup heavy cream
¼ teaspoon vanilla
0 calorie sweetener of choice equal to1 tablespoon sugar
4 ounces softened cream cheese
½ cup creamy natural peanut butter
0 calorie sweetener of choice equal to 4 tablespoons sugar

Preheat oven to 350° F. Combine ingredients for crust and press into bottom and sides of a 9" pie pan. Bake for 7 – 10 minutes until beginning to brown. Remove and set aside to cool. Beat cream, vanilla, and 1 tablespoon sweetener until stiff peaks form. Set aside. Combine cream cheese and peanut butter and beat on medium with an electric mixer until blended well. Add whipped cream mixture and 4 tablespoons sweetener to the peanut butter mixture and beat until smooth. Spread filling over pie crust and cover. Chill for minimum of 2 hours before serving. Cut into 8 slices.

Yield: 8 servings   Serving Size: 1 slice

Per Serving Using Peanuts:
Calories: 310.5; Fat: 28.1 g; Carb: 7.2 g; Dietary Fiber: 2.2 g; Sugar: 1.1 g; Protein: 8.9 g

Per Serving Using Almond Meal:
Calories: 307.0; Fat: 28.2 g; Carb: 7.4 g; Dietary Fiber: 2.4 g; Sugar: 1.0 g; Protein: 7.6 g

⚠ The caution sign identifies recipes that include caution items as ingredients. Some high fat caution items are milk, cheese, and nuts. Some high sugar (even though natural sugar) are pineapple and banana. Some high starchy vegetables are black beans and other legumes. These items are caution items for the 1st 3 weeks of maintenance. **Use these recipes in moderation and watch your morning weight closely, particularly during the 1st 3 weeks.**

Diet Tip: The maintenance phase of the HCG Protocol is NOT the Atkins diet. The major differences are that you can eat most fruits and vegetables whenever you like AND you are not encouraged to consistently eat foods with high fat content. Remember, you are training your new body to maintain your new weight – eat healthier to feel better, look better, and successfully lock in your new weight.

Apples with Vanilla Caramel Sauce

2½ cups sliced apples
0 calorie sweetener of choice equal to 1 cup sugar
2 tablespoons sugar free maple syrup
1 tablespoon cinnamon
2 tablespoons almond flour

Combine all ingredients and place in covered container overnight. Preheat oven to 350° F. Bake for 30 minutes until apples are done.

 Topping:
4 ounces Fiber One Vanilla Yogurt
1 ⅓ tablespoons Smucker's Sugar Free Caramel Sundae sauce
3 tablespoons chopped walnuts

To serve, divide baked apples evenly among 4 serving dishes. Over each dish, spoon 2 tablespoons yogurt over apples, drizzle 1 teaspoon caramel sauce on top of yogurt and sprinkle 2 teaspoons walnuts over top.

Yield: 4 servings
Per Serving: Calories: 125; Fat: 5.1 g; Carb: 26.8 g; Dietary Fiber: 4.6 g; Sugar: 9.9 g; Protein: 3.0 g

Crustless Pumpkin Pie

1¾ cups (small can) canned pumpkin
2 eggs
1 cup 2% milk
2 teaspoons cinnamon
½ teaspoon ginger
½ teaspoon nutmeg
0 calorie sweetener of choice equal to 1 cup sugar

Put all of the ingredients in a microwave safe bowl. Beat with a whisk to mix. Put in microwave uncovered. Cook on high for 8 – 10 minutes, depending on the power of your microwave. Check halfway through. Pie is done when the outside edges start to pull away from the sides. Insert a knife in the center, making sure it comes out clean. Take out of the microwave and cover bowl with a plate for 5 minutes. Serve warm or cold. Cut into 8 slices. Tastes great with a tablespoon of sugar free whipped topping.

Yield: 8 servings   Serving Size: 1 slice
Per Serving: Calories: 52; Fat: 1.9 g; Carb: 9.5 g; Dietary Fiber: 1.9 g; Sugar: 3.4 g; Protein: 3.0 g

2nd Three Weeks Recipes

Spicy Black Bean Salsa (2nd 3 Weeks Recipe)

1 can black beans, drained and rinsed
1 cup whole kernel corn, fresh or frozen
½ cup chopped ripe tomatoes
½ cup chopped cilantro
¼ cup chopped green onion
¼ cup chopped red onion
3 tablespoons vegetable oil
1 tablespoon ground cumin
½ cup fresh lime juice
Freshly ground black pepper to taste
Salt to taste

Combine beans, corn, cilantro, green onions, red onions, lime juice, oil, cumin, salt and pepper. Cover and chill 2-24 hours. Stir in tomatoes before serving.

Yield: 16 servings   Serving Size: ¼ cup
Per Serving: Calories: 127; Fat: 3.1 g; Carb: 19.7 g; Dietary Fiber: 4.5 g; Sugar: 1.3 g; Protein: 6.3 g

Taco Chips (2nd 3 Weeks Recipe

6 low carb wraps
1 packet taco seasoning mix
2 tablespoons water

Preheat oven to 350° F. Cut wraps like a pizza into 8 pieces. Mix taco seasoning with water. Place chips on baking sheet and brush the tops with the taco seasoned water. Bake for about 10 minutes until crisp. Cool before serving.

Yield: 6 servings   Serving Size: 1 wrap
Per Serving: Calories: 86; Fat: 1.8 g; Carb: 17.1 g; Dietary Fiber: 9.0 g; Sugar: 0.0 g; Protein: 6.4 g

Crazy Hi-Protein Chicken Wrap (2nd 3 Weeks Recipe)

8 ounces grilled chicken breast, sliced in strips
½ cup low fat 2% cottage cheese
½ cup salsa
1 chopped Roma tomato
2 slices Vidalia onion (chopped)
Dash each of salt, pepper & ground cumin
2 low carb wraps

Preheat oven to 400° F. In a medium bowl mix cottage cheese, salsa, tomato, onion, salt, pepper and cumin. Lay out tortillas and layer them first with the chicken, then the mixture. Wrap them up and bake in oven for 5 – 10 minutes. You can even microwave them in a pinch.

Yield: 2 servings
Per Serving: Calories: 335; Fat: 6.8; Carb: 22.3 g; Dietary Fiber: 10.6 g; Sugar: 3.4 g; Protein: 50.3 g

---

Lifestyle Tip: Be strong around family and friends. If you want to eat something unhealthy, that is one thing, but don't eat something unhealthy to make someone else feel better.

Cheesy Chicken (2nd 3 Weeks Recipe)

½ cup Baked Cheetos Puffs, crushed
2 (6 ounce) boneless skinless chicken breasts
Dash of salt
1 tablespoon olive oil

Roll chicken in crushed Cheetos and salt. Place in hot skillet with olive oil and cook about 15 minutes, until chicken is done. Note: This is also great baked.

Yield: 2 servings
Per Serving: Calories: 363; Fat: 19.7 g; Carb: 8.8 g; Dietary Fiber: 0.0 g; Sugar: 0.7 g; Protein: 34.2 g

Mashed Sweet Potatoes (2nd 3 Weeks Recipe)

2 large sweet potatoes
⅛ cup butter
¼ cup sugar free maple syrup
2 ½ teaspoons sea salt, divided

Preheat oven to 325° F. Peel potatoes and cut into large chunks. Add water, 2 teaspoons of sea salt, and peeled potato chunks to a pot. Boil sweet potatoes in water until fork easily pierces potatoes. Drain the water and return the pan to the warm burner but leave the burner turned off or on very low to avoid scorching the potatoes. Add the butter, syrup, and remaining ½ teaspoon salt to the pan. Mash the potatoes with an electric mixer or potato masher. Serve plain or with sweet butter and cinnamon.

Yield: 4 servings   Serving Size: approximately ½ cup
Per Serving: Calories: 132; Fat: 5.8 g; Carb: 20.8 g; Dietary Fiber: 2.3 g; Sugar: 4.0 g; Protein: 1.2 g

Festive Sweet Potato Casserole  (2nd 3 Weeks Recipe)

2 cups sweet potatoes, cooked and mashed
0 calorie sweetener of your choice equal to ½ cup sugar
⅓ cup milk
⅓ cup butter, melted
2 beaten eggs
1 teaspoon vanilla

Combine and mix well. Spoon into lightly greased 2 quart baking or casserole dish.

Topping:
0 calorie brown sugar sweetener of your choice equal to ½ cup brown sugar
¼ cup almond flour
¼ cup melted butter
½ cup chopped pecans

Preheat oven to 375° F. Combine topping ingredients and sprinkle on top of sweet potato mixture. Bake for 30 minutes or until goldn brown.

Yield: 6 servings
Per Serving: Calories: 336; Fat: 28.4 g; Carb: 18.9 g; Dietary Fiber: 3.4 g; Sugar: 1.7 g; Protein: 5.5 g

> ⚠ The caution sign identifies recipes that include caution items as ingredients. Some high fat caution items are milk, cheese, and nuts. Some high sugar (even though natural sugar) are pineapple and banana. Some high starchy vegetables are black beans and other legumes. These items are caution items for the 1st 3 weeks of maintenance. **Use these recipes in moderation and watch your morning weight closely, particularly during the 1st 3 weeks.**

Creamy Chocolate Layered Pie (2nd 3 Weeks Recipe)

Crust:

1 cup almond flour
3 tablespoons melted butter
0 calorie sweetener of choice equal to 5 tablespoons sugar
2 tablespoons cocoa powder

Press into pie plate and bake at 350 for 10 minutes. Cool.

Filling:

4 ounces softened ⅓ less fat cream cheese
1 tablespoon milk
0 calorie sweetener of choice equal to 1 tablespoon sugar
1 (12 ounce) tub sugar free whipped topping
1½ cups cold skim milk
2 small packages sugar free, fat free chocolate flavor instant pudding

Combine cream cheese, 1 tablespoon milk and sweetener in bowl and beat until smooth. Gently stir in 1 ½ cups of the whipped topping. Spread mixture on bottom of crust. Pour milk into a bowl and add pudding mix. Whisk for 1 minute, mix will be thick. Fold in 2 cups of the whipped topping. Spread over cream cheese layer and refrigerate for at least 4 hours before serving.

Yield: 8 servings
Per Serving: Calories: 282; Fat: 18.4g; Carb: 27.8 g; Dietary Fiber: 2.5 g; Sugar: 3.5 g; Protein: 5.9 g

Chocolate Peanut Butter Fluff  (2nd 3 Weeks Recipe)

1 large box sugar free, fat free chocolate instant pudding
3 cups skim milk
1 cup creamy peanut butter
½ tub (4 ounces) sugar free Cool Whip topping

Combine pudding and milk and beat for 2 minutes. Add peanut butter. Lightly fold in the Cool Whip and refrigerate. Chill for at least 10 minutes before serving.

Yield: 8 servings   Serving Size: ½ cup
Per Serving: Calories: 279; Fat: 18.1 g; Carb: 21.9 g; Dietary Fiber: 2.6 g; Sugar: 7.7 g; Protein: 11.6 g

Tasty Tip: For a special occasion, garnish with pieces of an Atkins Peanut Butter Cup.

⚠ The caution sign identifies recipes that include caution items as ingredients. Some high fat caution items are milk, cheese, and nuts. Some high sugar (even though natural sugar) are pineapple and banana. Some high starchy vegetables are black beans and other legumes. These items are caution items for the 1st 3 weeks of maintenance. **Use these recipes in moderation and watch your morning weight closely, particularly during the 1st 3 weeks.**

Pecan Pie (2nd 3 Weeks Recipe)

Crust:

¾ cup almond meal

¼ cup finely chopped pecans

2 tablespoons melted butter

0 calorie sweetener of choice equal to 2 tablespoons sugar

Filling:

1½ cups sugar free maple syrup

4 eggs

0 calorie sweetener of choice equal to ½ cup sugar

5 tablespoons butter

1 teaspoon vanilla

2 cups chopped pecans

Preheat oven to 325° F. Combine ingredients for crust and press into bottom and sides of a 9" pie pan. Bake for 7 – 10 minutes until beginning to brown. Remove and set aside to cool. Increase oven temperature to 375° F.

Simmer syrup in a saucepan. Cook about 10 minutes, until reduced by half. Cool to room temperature. Melt butter, and then cool slightly. Whisk eggs, ½ cup sweetener, butter and vanilla. Whisk in cooled syrup and add pecans. Pour mixture into crust. Bake for at least 30 minutes until edges are firm. Center will be less firm. Cool on wire rack. Slice into 12 pieces.

Yield: 12 servings
Per Serving: Calories: 328; Fat: 30.8 g; Carb: 13.4 g; Dietary Fiber: 3.2 g; Sugar: 8.6 g; Protein: 6.0 g

⚠ The caution sign identifies recipes that include caution items as ingredients. Some high fat caution items are milk, cheese, and nuts. Some high sugar (even though natural sugar) are pineapple and banana. Some high starchy vegetables are black beans and other legumes. These items are caution items for the 1st 3 weeks of maintenance. **Use these recipes in moderation and watch your morning weight closely, particularly during the 1st 3 weeks.**

Index